On Wine and Hashish

On Wine and Hashish

Charles Baudelaire

Translated by Andrew Brown

.

ET REMOTISSIMA PROPE

Hesperus Classics

Hesperus Classics
Published by Hesperus Press Limited
4 Rickett Street, London SW6 1RU
www.hesperuspress.com

First published by Hesperus Press Limited, 2002
Reprinted 2007

Introduction and English language translation © Andrew Brown, 2002
Foreword © Margaret Drabble, 2002

Designed and typeset by Fraser Muggeridge studio
Printed in Jordan by Jordan National Press

ISBN: 1-84391-017-9
ISBN13: 978-1-84391-017-6

CONTENTS

For the English reader, Baudelaire represents the essence of Paris, and of the French aesthetic. His Paris is the Paris of grandeur and squalor, of gutters and garrets, of faded palaces hung with tattered finery, of sculptured nymphs and formal gardens and flowing fountains. It is the Paris of absinthe, of wine, and of opium. This is, of course, a mythical Paris, an artificial paradise of a Paris. But is also an artificially, artistically heightened version of the real thing, of the real place and the real palace of art.

In his essays, poems and prose poems on the theme of *Les Paradis artificiels*, Baudelaire manifests an extraordinarily complex and ambivalent attitude towards the truth and the artifice of artistic creation, and towards the various paths to paradise. The essays here presented, in a fine new translation by Andrew Brown, deal principally with the distortions and intensifications of perception induced by wine and hashish. (Opium lurks in the subtext.) The topicality of this theme, in an age even more obsessed than his own by the drug culture, is obvious. Some of our younger writers have been grouped under the label of 'the chemical generation', and not a day goes by without some newspaper story about the dangers (and occasionally the delights) of cannabis, ecstasy, heroin or cocaine. These younger writers follow on in an old tradition, which in England goes back to the days of Coleridge, De Quincey, Wilkie Collins, and many others. Coleridge's vision of Xanadu, with its caverns measureless to man and its caves of ice, may have been inspired by opium, and it certainly bears a resemblance to some of the visions of the hashish-takers of the Hotel Pimodan in Paris, and to the architectural and spatial fantasies described here by Baudelaire.

Is Baudelaire an apologist for artificial stimulants? There is no simple answer to this, and the reader will have to weigh the evidence. We know that one of his most passionately asserted maxims was '*Enivrez-vous!*': in the short prose poem of this title he urges us to be ever drunk, by whatever means we choose – on wine, on poetry, or on virtue, it matters not, for only through drunkenness do we escape from the tyranny of time.

Wine, in fact – the most Parisian, the most native of his inebriating recommendations – comes out best from these eulogies: there is a reckless, full-blooded Dionysian enthusiasm in his praise of the effects of alcohol. He sees it as a social, comradely and invigorating stimulant, readily available to the poor: it is the chosen balm of the people, in its spirit essentially levelling and democratic. It can deposit any of us, happily, in the gutter, or inspire the dullest of us to flights of oratory or music. Wine, he suggests, is our divine right, and it is good for us. Few would wish to argue with that.

The question of his attitude to hashish is much more problematic, and he issues several somewhat contradictory warnings against indulgence and addiction. He seems to think of it as a less 'natural' substance than the juice of the grape, and it is certainly true that hashish-producing hemp was not at that period (and for all I know is not now) grown in France: the hashish taken by those whose experiences are described here was imported. Yet his account of the indirect, intoxicating, natural effects of lucerne and hemp on harvesters, or even on children rolling in meadows of grass, seems to gainsay his desire to contrast the natural and the chemical. Also, we need not necessarily accept his view that hashish-takers are characteristically indolent, antisocial and work-shy, compared with hard-labouring patriotic French drunkards. These racial stereotypes do not bear examination now, and did not then. They are part of another agenda.

Paris has long been, for the English, an exotic, erotic and romantic city, a city where inhibitions vanish and dreams are fulfilled. For Baudelaire's generation the Orient represented a similar mirage of freedom. 'Orientalism', as notably redefined by Edward W. Said in *Orientalism: Western Conceptions of the Orient* (1978), was an attitude of mind, rather than a geographical location, and it drew to it many of the French Romantics, including Flaubert, de Nerval, Gautier and Baudelaire. Baudelaire himself made one somewhat abortive voyage eastwards as a young man in 1841, setting out on a packet-boat for Calcutta but returning when he reached Mauritius and Ile de Réunion: this journey was undertaken through family pressure, partly in order to rescue him from bad company and the perils of the streets of Paris, and it may, ironically, have introduced him to the perils of hashish.

He renewed or pursued his acquaintance with this substance on his return to France, in 1845, in the company of other literary and artistic members of 'Le Club des hachichins'. This club met at the Hotel Pimodan, a grand, large and still extant mansion (not a hotel in the English sense of the word) on the quai d'Anjou on the Ile Saint-Louis in Paris, where in 1843, the poet had taken a small mansard apartment. At this time, hashish was still a foreign and exotic drug: even the spelling of the word was undetermined, and Baudelaire describes with a somewhat cautious respect the preferred methods of administering this 'green jelly'. It could, as he makes clear, have incalculable and unpredictable physical and mental consequences. Its psychopharmacological properties were already being tentatively explored by medical practitioners, but these properties were by no means fully understood. Unlike wine, it was a novelty and a mystery.

Hashish provided a voyage into the imaginary Orient, a trip into the unknown. What emerges most powerfully from these essays is the effect it had on Baudelaire's poetic imagination. It is hashish, not wine, which seems to raise him to the greatest eloquence. He reveals to us enchanting and visionary landscapes, and beguiles us with vegetable correspondences, musical transformations, and watery expanses. But it is a theatrical, gilded, and essentially urban vision of nature, of which artifice is an essential component. It is a Parisian version of William Blake's English mysticism: in *The Marriage of Heaven and Hell* Blake told us that 'if the doors of perception were cleansed everything would appear to man as it is, infinite.' Baudelaire reveals infinity to us through endless distortions and refractions. He leads us into its golden cage and its mirrored maze, but he warns us, as we enter, that it is dangerous, as well as beautiful.

– Margaret Drabble, 2002

In 1882 there appeared, in the journal *Mind* (vol. 7) an article on the 'Subjective Effect of Nitrous Oxide' by the American philosopher William James. He was to look back on his experiment with the gas, performed partly out of scientific curiosity, as one of the most overwhelming experiences of his life. He referred to 'the tremendously exciting sense of an intense metaphysical illumination', and in his 1902 study, *The Varieties of Religious Experience*, remarked that in the trance induced by the gas, we may have 'a genuine metaphysical revelation' akin to mystical insight. He also dwelt on the ineffability of the experience: his *Mind* article had already noted that 'as sobriety returns, the feeling of insight fades, and one is left staring vacantly at a few disjointed words and phrases... I have sheet after sheet of phrases dictated or written during the intoxication, which to the sober reader seem meaningless drivel, but which at the moment of transcribing were fused in the fire of infinite rationality'. His jottings included: 'That sounds like nonsense, but it's pure *on* sense!'; 'medical school; divinity school, school! SCHOOL! Oh my God, oh God; oh God!'; and 'there are no differences but differences of degree between different degrees of difference and no difference' – after which it comes as no surprise that he speculated that Hegel, of whom this last sentence sounds like a parody, might have reached a similar state of intoxication, although using pure thought rather than nitrous oxide.

Baudelaire took hashish at the Hotel Pimodan in Paris, where Dr Moreau de Tours organised his famous 'fantasias' for those who wanted to sample the drug under his medical supervision. They included Théophile Gautier, who in his 'Le

Club des hachichins' (1846: Baudelaire knew this essay) gives us a more personal and detailed account of one of these sessions. Gautier claimed that Baudelaire attended more as a spectator than a partaker, and there is indeed something rather impersonal about Baudelaire's own evocation of the hashish experience. The drug seems to have left him relatively indifferent, unlike opium, to which he would become addicted – though even here, he chose to write about his encounter with the stimulant by translating and commenting on passages from Thomas De Quincey's *Confessions of an English Opium Eater* (1822). There is something mediated and intertextual about all Baudelaire's writings on intoxicants. A kind of modesty is perhaps at work here: boasting about one's glorious visions, the intensity of one's sensations, and their ineffable incommunicability is not something a dandy does. Nor does an artist: like the actor according to Denis Diderot, coolly calculating his effects so as to transmit emotion all the more powerfully to his audience, Baudelaire does not believe in effusiveness. (On another level, but for similar reasons, he was attracted to the alluring artistry of the frigid, or apparently frigid, courtesan.) So, being himself a relatively abstemious consumer of alcohol, he fills his essay on wine with third-person anecdotes and seems to be celebrating it vicariously through its effect on others, in particular the poor. There is indeed a political slant in the way 'On Wine and Hashish' praises wine and denigrates hashish: wine, a product of human labour, is the well-deserved reward of the labouring classes, while hashish is for idle dilettantes. There is a trace here of Baudelaire's republican fraternity with the workers' revolts of 1848–51: there is also, as throughout his writing on intoxicants, an argument with himself. The Baudelaire who exalts the sociability and conviviality of wine, its ability to fortify one's strength and will, and who criticises the 'hash-ishin' as lazy, solipsistic and self-absorbed, viewed himself as a neurasthenic idler, and in his pose as a solitary dandy living in front of a mirror, commented that the more friends you have, the more pairs of gloves you need, as you never know what you might pick up.

The series of oppositions between wine and hashish (wine is more natural, hashish more artificial; wine is sociable and hashish egotistic; wine is hard-working and hashish indolent) is in any case perfectly tendentious (hashish is no more arti-ficial than wine; hashish can be enjoyed in company whereas solitary boozers are commonplace; and alcohol is not always conducive to outbursts of productive labour). Nor is it clear which of them is best at 'multiplying individuality' – the overt theme of the essay as signalled by its subtitle – or even whether this was necessarily, for Baudelaire, a good thing. There was a Baudelaire who longed, like the hashish-takers he depicts, to escape from self into pantheistic absorption, a reverie in which the distinction between subject and object is overcome and time suspended: this at least was one escape route from the prison of self and the menacing tick of the clock (Baudelaire contracted a venereal illness in 1839, and despite moments of apparent nonchalance was rarely unaware of the slow but implacable ascent of tabes dorsalis up his spine – it was after all to alleviate the pains of syphilis that he first resorted to opium). It was this Baudelaire who enjoyed taking 'a bath in the crowd', plunging into the multitude of Parisian pleasure-seekers and strollers, or identifying vicariously with anony-mous passers-by and the often isolated, downtrodden figures haunting the boulevards and public gardens. But there was another Baudelaire who longed, not to multiply individuality, but to be *one*, even at the price of solitude: who cultivated distance, difference, the aloofness of the dandy. It was this latter Baudelaire who was also the aesthete, preferring the indirect communication of art to the mere transcription of experience. We have seen how comic were James' attempts to verbalise his nitrous-oxide trance: Baudelaire remarks on the frenzied punning that the 'hashishin' were prone to, their fits of the giggles, and the way the deeper absorption of kief resists linguistic depiction. (In 1841, Dr Moreau was reduced to repetitious platitude in *his* depiction of the effect of hashish as 'a feeling of physical and mental well-being, inner contentment, intimate joy, well-being, contentment, indefinable joy that you seek in vain to understand or analyse'.) He does try to pattern his account and to convey something of the euphoria of hashish, but real ecstasy (and the equally real nightmares induced by drugs which, though referred to in his reworking of De Quincey, are absent from his writing on hashish) is to be found more in the aesthetic control (and the fictional distancing) of his cycle of poems *Les Fleurs du Mal* (*The Flowers of Evil*).

Like everyone who resorts to drink or drugs, Baudelaire did so for many reasons: curiosity, the need to escape, an attempt to revive flagging inspiration, the desire to numb physical or mental pain (eventually including that caused by the guilt of being an addict), a longing for heightened awareness, and even the yearning for transcendence. In *The Varieties of Religious Experience*, William James was to write lyrically of the mystical visions vouchsafed by intoxicants: 'The sway of alcohol over mankind is unquestionably due to its power to stimulate the mystical faculties of human nature, usually crushed to earth by the cold facts and dry criticisms of the sober hour. Sobriety diminishes, discriminates, and says no; drunkenness expands, unites, and says yes'.

It does indeed: yes, and again yes; just another glass, just another fix – though to be fair neither James nor Baudelaire are interested, as writers, in the problem of addiction as such. Or rather, Baudelaire was addicted to many other things. Though one of his *Petits poèmes en prose* (*Little Poems in Prose*) is called '*Enivrez-vous!*' ('Get Drunk!'), it tells us that our intoxicant of choice can be wine, virtue, or poetry. Baudelaire was too addicted to poetry (and perhaps, in his way, virtue) for his dependence on wine, or rather stimulants, not to be a problem, for if they gave desire (for visions of beauty and escape) they threatened to take away performance (the ability to produce a finished work of art that would encapsulate those visions). Drugs pandered to a need for beauty that they also, in the long term, frustrated. Baudelaire shows, in fact, how all the reasons for resorting to drugs mentioned above are linked, and this enables him to give a more nuanced account of the ethics of their use than James, for whom the mystical experience is important in itself, whether or not it can be verbally conveyed (especially because, in fact, it cannot). It is because Baudelaire was an artist that he could not spend all his time stoned: aesthetics and ethics melded here as everywhere else in his work. When he criticises drug use, it is not from the standpoint of the 'Pharisaical pseudo-moralists' he rebukes in 'On Wine and Hashish' who think they have all they need in the real world and don't need to see life through the bottom of a glass – and thus decide that the poor, who don't have what they need, shouldn't be allowed to drown their sorrows either. But it is as a moralist that, in the lectures he gave in Brussels to advertise his *Les Paradis artificiels* (*Artificial Paradises* – the writings on wine and hashish plus his adaptation of De Quincey), he informed his audience that stimulants tend 'to produce a debilitating effect in proportion to the stimulus, and a retribution as cruel as the pleasure was intense', and 'seekers after paradise are creating their own hell, preparing it and digging it with a success which, if they could only foresee it, would perhaps terrify them'. Not just because of the hangover, or the pains of addiction – by making you suffer, these might even have a salutary effect – rather because, for Baudelaire, nothing was worse than thinking you could win paradise easily. A perpetual procrastinator, convinced of his own weakness of will, permanently prone to what he called 'the malady of monks', accidie (sloth, depression, despair), he came to see drugs as a form of cheap transcendence. Flaubert, who took the more scientific view that the effect of drugs should be discussed more neutrally, was surprised at Baudelaire's 'Catholic' denunciation of them: Baudelaire replied that, yes, in the teeth of his whole century, he could not fail to think that there was something diabolical in the promptings from outside that he associated with drugs. (That drugs might be diabolical is perhaps what led the devil-worshipping Aleister Crowley, 'the wickedest man in the world', to translate 'The Poem of Hashish'.)

Drugs were perhaps too natural for Baudelaire: artificial paradises but, for this lover of the artificial, not artificial enough. And not transcendent enough for someone who set transcendence very high – so high as to be found only 'out of this world', as another prose poem puts it. He would have suspected as possibly devilish the mystical visions reported by James: what if they were *false epiphanies*? What if the 'doors of perception' that Aldous Huxley claimed were opened by mescaline and LSD led to a sense of oneness with the universe that was a subtle form of narcissism? No one charted more than Baudelaire the desperate human need to transcend the given: *Les Fleurs du Mal* tries out so many of the emergency exits (love and beauty; the ironic fraternity to be found in the big city; wine; perversion; blasphemy; death) leading from a world which seems to have screwed the lid down tight on all human aspirations. And try to imagine a society in which one would *never* need to escape (if only into dreams). There must surely be, if not doors, at least windows on otherness. Baudelaire's work is full of them. The window gives you the opportunity for reverie: from outside, you see a figure at a window and imagine (without bothering to find out how true your imaginings are) a whole life story; or, from inside, you gaze down from your window (in a Paris garret, of course) at the panorama of the city, or up at that framed infinitude, the sky. The window offers an escape, like intoxicants. But Baudelaire shows how often the window becomes a mirror: the dreamer finds no real escape, but simply his own self, however imaginatively multiplied, looking back at him. Likewise, both wine and hashish may seem to offer us transcendence. But 'wine is similar to man' ('On Wine and Hashish'), simply enlarging virtues and vices that are already there; and hashish is a mirror – 'a magnifying mirror, but still just a mirror' ('The Poem of Hashish'). There is a curious formal counterpart to this specular theme running throughout Baudelaire's work: its proneness to doubling. Some of the material of 'On Wine and Hashish' is echoed, with minor variations, in 'The Poem of Hashish'. (In a note of 1869, Baudelaire remarked that he had not been over-scrupulous about 'copying himself at ten years' distance', and the 'double use' of the same material was necessary to preserve the integrity of the texts.) The prose of 'On Wine and Hashish' is mirrored by two poems in *The Flowers of Evil*: *'L'Âme du Vin'* ['The Soul of Wine'] and *'Le Vin des Chiffonniers.'*

['The Rag-pickers' Wine']). Furthermore, several other of the poems in the *Flowers* have a prose double in the *Little Poems in Prose*. It is as if Baudelaire's very singularity (*'singulier'*, meaning both numerically single, and strange, is a key word in his aesthetics) was also a duplicity, a longing to say everything twice over. His accounts of meeting doubles of his own alienation wherever he goes, his address to the reader of *Les Fleurs du Mal* ('hypocritical reader! my fellow man! my brother!') add to the effect: poetry, like intoxicants, seems to offer multiplicity and fusion, but collapses, or wilfully withdraws, into a specular tête-à-tête. Baudelaire's work can be a hall of mirrors – fatefully so. In 1864, at the start of his disastrous lecture-tour of Belgium, he put up at the Grand Hôtel du Miroir in Brussels; at the end of his life, just three years later, stricken with aphasia and semi-paralysis, he bowed to his own image in a mirror as if it were a stranger.

Baudelaire was right to see drugs as a matter of more than physiology. This should not be allowed to undermine the attractiveness of his presentation of the hashish experience. The histrionic laughter at the Hotel Pimodan, and the mellowness of mood among the 'hashishin' are alluring enough, though not very far from the dope-head or piss artist's corny mateyness (often the inverted mirror-image of real aggression). The exaggerated politeness and fastidious solicitude of the hashish-taker, the phobia about hurting anyone's feelings to the slightest degree, is pleasantly comic: it was an effect also noted by the great Jewish-German critic Walter Benjamin who wrote with such empathy on Baudelaire as to seem, at times, a reincarnation of him. Scrutinising the menu in a Marseilles restaurant while under the influence of hashish, Benjamin found that he simply had to order everything on the menu, so as not to offend any of the dishes by a refusal: he felt an unusual sense of fraternity – 'all men are brothers' – with complete strangers in the streets ('Hashish in Marseilles'). But for Baudelaire, all this (even the mystical overcoming of subjectivity in the deeper states of trance) is a mere rococo of feelings as opposed to the sombre baroque struggle his work as a whole recounts – that against accidie. He sometimes lived like a dandy, and the dandy, in his view, 'does nothing': but he also claimed that a procrastinator awoken every morning by a man with a whip, and driven to work by fear if not pleasure, would have to count that tormentor his truest friend. That the glimpses of eternity afforded by drugs might be robbing him of real time, and their intimations of the infinite destroying his capacity for finitude, became a frightening leitmotif in his *Journaux intimes* (*Intimate Journals*) once he realised – 'today, 23 January 1862, I have been administered a singular warning, I have felt passing over me *the wind of the wing of imbecility*' – that time was running out. The main question now was not whether his intoxicant of choice would be wine or hashish, but how long he could survive as a productive artist, given the increasing mental paralysis that drugs merely fostered. There are two ways of escaping from time, he wrote in *Mon Coeur mis à nu* (*My Heart Laid Bare*): pleasure and work. 'Pleasure wears us down. Work fortifies us. Let us choose.' Drugs meant pleasure. So he decided against them – though in terms curiously suggesting that work itself might be a new escape from time, and thus a new drug. The last pages of his *Intimate Journals* are filled with the self-flagellating maxims ('if you worked every day, life would be more tolerable for you' – 'Too late perhaps!' – 'Immediate work, even if it's no good, is better than daydreaming') of the aspirant workaholic. Almost the last words of the journals announce the self-denying ordinance 'to obey the principles of the strictest sobriety, the first of which is the suppression of every kind of stimulant whatsoever'. Perhaps this was impossible for someone like Baudelaire – perhaps it is ultimately impossible for anyone: even at our most sober, we are always intoxicated by some delicious poison or other, in thrall to some voluptuous or austere addiction. 'Get Drunk!' as the prose poem puts it – 'on wine, virtue, or poetry: take your pick'.

– Andrew Brown, 2002

Note on Publication Dates:
'On Wine and Hashish' ('*Du Vin et du hachisch*') was first published in the *Messager de l'Assemblée*, in March 1851. 'The Poem of Hashish' ('*Le Poème du hachisch*') was published in *Les Paradis artificiels*, 1860.

This translation is from the 'Pléiade' edition of Baudelaire's *Oeuvres complètes* (2 vols: vol. 1), edited by Claude Pichois (Gallimard: Paris, 1975).

On Wine and Hashish

Compared as a Means
of Multiplying Individuality

1
WINE

A very famous man, who was at the same time a great fool –
two things which apparently go very well together, as I will
doubtless have on more than one occasion the painful
pleasure of demonstrating – has had the temerity, in a book on
the delights of gastronomy, composed from the twofold point
of view of hygiene and pleasure, to write the following under
the article WINE: 'The patriarch Noah is considered to be
the inventor of wine; it is a liquor made from the fruit of the
vine.'

And then? Then, nothing: that's all there is. However much
you leaf through the volume, turn it this way and that, read it
upside down, back to front, from right to left and from left to
right, you won't find anything else on wine in the *Physiology of
Taste* by the most illustrious and respected Brillat-Savarin:
'*The patriarch Noah…*' and '*it is a liquor…*' [1]

I can imagine how an inhabitant of the moon or some
distant planet, travelling through our world, and worn out by
his long journeys, might desire to refresh his palate and warm
up his stomach. He is eager to find out about the pleasures and
customs of our earth. He has vaguely heard of delicious
liquors with which the citizens of this globe procured for
themselves as much courage and gaiety as they wanted. So as
to be more sure of his choice, the inhabitant of the moon
consults the oracle of taste, the celebrated and infallible Brillat-
Savarin, and there he finds, under the article WINE, this
invaluable piece of information: '*The patriarch Noah…*' and
'*this liquor is made…*' That is bound to get his digestive juices
flowing. That really explains things well. It is impossible, once
you have read those words, not to have a clear and correct idea

of all wines, their different qualities, their disadvantages, their effects on the stomach and the brain.

Ah! dear friends, don't read Brillat-Savarin. *May God preserve those he loves from reading useless books*; this is the first maxim in a little book by Lavater, a philosopher who loved mankind more than all the magistrates of the ancient and modern world ever did.[2] No cake has been baptised with the name of Lavater; but the memory of that angelic man will still live on among Christians, when the worthy burghers themselves have forgotten the *Brillat-Savarin*, a kind of insipid brioche the least failing of which is that it acts as a pretext for people to spout a number of inanely pedantic maxims drawn from the well-known masterpiece.

If a new edition of that phoney masterpiece ever dares to brave the common sense of modern humanity, melancholy drinkers, merry drinkers, all you who seek in wine memory or oblivion, and who, never finding it as perfect as you would wish, contemplate the sky only through the bottom of a bottle*, forgotten and neglected drinkers, will you buy a copy and render good for evil, benevolence for indifference?

I open the divine Hoffmann's *Kreisleriana*[4], and there I read a curious recommendation. The conscientious musician must help himself to champagne if he wants to compose a comic opera. In it he will find the foamy and light-hearted gaiety the genre requires. Religious music needs Rhenish or Jurançon. As at the bottom of profound ideas, an intoxicating bitterness lurks in it; but heroic music cannot do without Burgundy. It has the earnest ardour and the enthusiasm of patriotism. That is certainly an advantage, and apart from the passionate feelings of a drinker, I find in this remark an impartiality which does the greatest honour to a German.

* Béroalde de Verville, *Art de parvenir*.[3]

Hoffmann had set up a strange psychological barometer designed to indicate the different temperatures and atmospheric phenomena of his soul. On it you come across gradations such as these: a somewhat ironic spirit tempered by indulgence; the spirit of solitude and profound contentment with yourself; musical gaiety, musical enthusiasm, musical tempestuousness, sarcastic gaiety intolerable to yourself, a longing to escape from your *self*, excessive objectivity, fusion of your being with nature. It goes without saying that the gradations of Hoffmann's mental barometer were determined on the basis of the order in which they are produced, as in ordinary barometers. It seems to me that between this psychic barometer and the explanation of the musical qualities of different wines, there is an obvious fraternity.

Hoffmann, when death came to carry him off, was just starting to make money. Fortune was smiling on him. Like our own dear and great Balzac, it was only towards the end of life that he saw the aurora borealis of his oldest hopes shining. At that time, publishers, who fought over his tales for their journals, habitually added, in the hope of thereby getting into his good books, a case of French wines to the payments they sent him.

2

Who has never known you, O profound joys of wine? Whoever has had a remorse to appease, a memory to evoke, a sorrow to drown, a castle in the air to build, all, in short, have called on you, the mysterious god hidden in the fibres of the vine. How splendid the great displays put on by wine are, and lit by the light of the inner sun! How genuine and fervent is that second youth which man can draw from it! But how fearsome too are its lightning-bolts of pleasure and its debilitating charms. And yet tell me, on your souls and your consciences, judges, legislators, men of the world, all you who are mellowed by happiness, all you whose good fortune means that virtue and health come easily to you, tell me, who among you will have the implacable strength of mind to condemn the man whose genius comes from drink?

Wine, moreover, is not always a terrible wrestler assured of his victory, and sworn to have neither pity nor mercy. Wine is similar to man: we will never know how much we can esteem him or despise him, love him or hate him, nor how many sublime actions or monstrous crimes he is capable of. So let us not be crueller towards wine than we are towards ourselves, and let us treat him as our equal.

It sometimes seems to me that I can hear wine talking – he speaks with his soul, with that voice of the spirits which only spirits can hear and understand – and says: 'Man, my beloved, I want to sing out to you, despite my prison of glass and my bolts of cork, a song full of fraternity, a song full of joy, light and hope. I am not ungrateful; I know I owe my life to you. I know how much labour it cost you, and how long you endured the sun's heat on your back. You gave me life, and I will reward you. I will pay off my debt to the full; for I feel an extraordinary joy when I tumble deep down a throat parched by hard work. The breast of a decent man is a dwelling-place that I far prefer to these melancholy and impassive cellars. It is a joyous tomb in which I eagerly accomplish my destiny. I make a great commotion in the worker's stomach, and from there by invisible staircases I slip up to his brain where I perform my sublime dance.

'Can you hear stirring in me the echo of the powerful refrains of old times, the songs of love and glory? I am the soul of the fatherland, I am half lover, half soldier. I am the hope of Sundays. Work makes weekdays prosperous, wine makes Sundays happy. Elbows on the family table and sleeves rolled up, you will proudly sing my praises, and you will be filled with contentment.

'I will bring a twinkle to the eyes of your old woman, the old companion of your daily sorrows and of your oldest hopes. I will impart tenderness to her glances and I will let the sparkle of youth gleam again from the depths of her eyes. And as for your dear little son, all pale and wan, that poor little donkey harnessed to the same exhausting tasks as the shaft-horse, I will restore to him the healthy glow of the baby's cradle, and I will be for this new athlete entering life's arena the oil that firmed up the muscles of wrestlers in ancient times.

'I will drop to the depths of your breast like an organic elixir. I will be the seed that fertilises the laboriously dug furrow. Our intimate commingling will create poetry. Between the two of us we will produce a god, and flutter off into the infinite, like birds, butterflies, gossamer threads, perfumes, and all winged things.'

'That is what wine sings in its mysterious language. Woe betide the man whose selfish heart, closed to the sorrows of his brothers, has never heard this song!

I've often thought that if Jesus Christ were to appear today in the dock, some prosecutor would turn up to urge that his case is aggravated by the fact that this is not his first offence. As for wine, it renews its offence every day. Every day it repeats its benefits. This is doubtless the explanation for the relentless hostility moralists show towards it. When I say moralists, I mean Pharisaical pseudo-moralists.

But there's something else we need to consider. Let's lower our sights a little. Let's contemplate one of those mysterious beings, living so to speak off the excrement of great cities; for there are some strange occupations around. There's a huge number of them. I've sometimes thought with terror that there were occupations that brought no joy, trades without pleasure, labours without relaxation, pains without compensation. I was wrong. Here is a man whose task it is to pick up all the rubbish produced on one day in the capital. All that the great city has thrown out, all it has lost, all it has disdained, all it has broken, he catalogues and collects. He consults the archives of debauchery, works through the lumber-room of rubbish. He makes a selection, chooses astutely; he picks up, as a miser seizes on treasure, the refuse which, when chewed over by the divinity of Industry, will become objects of use or enjoyment. Look at him, in the dark glow of the street lamps whose light flickers fitfully in the night wind, climbing up one of the long winding roads lined with small dwellings on the Montagne Sainte-Geneviève. He is wearing his wickerwork shawl with his number seven[5]. He arrives, wagging his head and stumbling over the cobbles like those young poets who spend all their days wandering around in search of rhymes. He is talking to himself; he pours out his soul to the dark cold night air. It's a splendid monologue that puts to shame the most lyrical tragedies. 'Forward march! Division, vanguard, army!' Exactly like Bonaparte dying on St Helena! It seems that number seven has changed into a sceptre of iron, and the wicker shawl into an imperial mantle. Now he is complimenting his army. The battle is won, but it was a heated exchange. He passes on horseback beneath the triumphal arches. His heart swells with happiness. He listens with delight to the acclamations of an enthusiastic public. Any moment now he will be dictating a law code superior to all codes known hitherto. He swears solemnly that he will make his peoples happy. Wretchedness and vice have disappeared from humanity.

And yet his back is rubbed raw from top to bottom by the weight of the basket he carries. He is harassed by domestic worries. He is ground down by forty years of hard work and running around. Old age torments him. But wine, like a new Pactolus[6], sweeps its waves of intellectual gold across languishing mankind. Like good kings, it rules by serving its people, and it sings its exploits through its subjects' throats.

There is on the world's round surface a numberless, nameless throng who could never find enough alleviation for their sufferings in sleep. Wine composes songs and poems for them.

Many will doubtless find me too indulgent. 'You're excusing drunkenness, you're idealising dissoluteness.' I admit that faced with these benefits I don't have the heart to enumerate any negative points. In any case, I have already said that wine was comparable to man, I have granted that in both cases their crimes were equal to their virtues. Can I do more? And another idea occurs to me. If wine were to disappear from human production, I believe that in the health and the intellect of the planet there would be left a void, an absence, a defect much more dreadful than all the excesses and the deviant behaviour for which wine is held responsible. Isn't it reasonable to think that men who never drink wine, whether out of naivety or on principle, are imbeciles or hypocrites – imbeciles, in other words, men unacquainted with humanity or nature, artists spurning the traditional means of art, workers blaspheming against mechanics; and hypocrites, in other words, closet guzzlers, braggarts of sobriety, drinking on the sly and keeping for themselves some occult wine? A man who drinks only water has a secret to hide from his fellow men.

Let the reader judge: a few years ago, at an exhibition of

painting, the crowd of imbeciles rioted in front of a picture polished, waxed, and varnished like an industrial object. It was the absolute antithesis of art; it was to Drolling's Kitchen[7] what madness is to stupidity, or true zealots to a lukewarm follower. In this microscopic painting you could see a whole swarm of flies. I was drawn to this monstrous object like everyone else, but I was ashamed of yielding to this strange temptation, based on the irresistible allure of the horrible. Finally, I realised that I was drawn to it unwittingly by a philosophical sense of curiosity, the immense desire to know the moral character of the man who could have committed such a criminal absurdity. I made a wager with myself that he must be fundamentally wicked. I made enquiries, and my instinct had the pleasure of winning this psychological wager. I learnt that the monster got up regularly before daybreak, that he had ruined his housekeeper, and *that he only ever drank milk!*

One or two more stories, and then we will make some dogmatic pronouncements. One day, on the pavement, I saw a big gathering; I managed to peer over the shoulders of the curious onlookers, and this is what I saw: a man lying stretched out on his back, his eyes open and staring at the sky, another man, standing in front of him, and communicating with him just by gestures, the man on the ground replying to him just with his eyes, both of them seemingly animated by a tremendous benevolence. The gestures of the man standing were saying to the intelligence of the man lying down: 'Come on, a bit further, happiness is just there, two steps away, come along to the corner of the street. We haven't completely lost sight of the shores of woe, we're still not out on the high seas of reverie; come on now, get your strength up, friend, tell your legs to obey your mind.'

All this was accompanied by rhythmical wobblings and

swayings. The other had in fact doubtless reached the *high seas* (and he was in reality sailing in the gutter), for his beatific smile said in reply: 'Leave your friend alone. The shore of woe has disappeared quite far enough behind the beneficent fogs; I have nothing further to ask from the heaven of reverie.' I even believe I heard a vague phrase, or rather a sigh loosely formulated into words escaping from his mouth: 'You have to be sensible.' This is the height of sublimity. But in drunkenness there is a hyper-sublime, as you are about to see. His ever-indulgent friend headed off alone to the tavern, then returned with a piece of rope in his hands. Doubtless he couldn't stand the idea of sailing off by himself and pursuing his happiness all alone; that is why he had come back for his friend in a carriage. The carriage was the rope; he passed the carriage round his waist. His friend smiled as he lay there: he had doubtless understood this maternal idea. The other one tied a knot; then he trotted away, like a gentle, discreet horse, carting off his friend to where happiness awaited him. The man being carted off, or rather dragged away and polishing the cobbles with his back as he went, was still smiling his ineffable smile.

The crowd remained stupefied; for everything that is too beautiful, that surpasses man's poetic strength, produces more astonishment than real feeling.

There was a man, a Spaniard, a guitarist who spent a long time travelling with Paganini; it was before the latter officially became a great celebrity.

Both of them led the grand nomadic life of gypsies, itinerant musicians, people without family and without fatherland. Both of them, violinist and guitarist, gave concerts everywhere they went. In this way they wandered for some time through different countries. My Spaniard had such a talent that like Orpheus he could say: 'I am the master of nature'.

Wherever he went, strumming away on his guitar so that its strings twanged harmoniously under his thumb, he was certain to be followed by a crowd. With a secret like that you run no risk of dying of starvation. They followed him as if he were Jesus Christ. How can anyone refuse to give dinner and hospitality to the man, the genius, the sorcerer who has made your soul sing its most beautiful, most secret, most unknown, most mysterious arias! I have been assured that this man, although playing an instrument which produces only successive sounds, easily managed to produce continuous sounds. Paganini held the purse-strings; he managed the public funds, which will surprise nobody.

The money box travelled on the person of its keeper; sometimes it was up above, sometimes down below, one day in his boots, the following between two seams of his garment. When the guitarist, who was a real tippler, asked how things stood financially, Paganini replied that there was nothing left, at least almost nothing; for Paganini was like old people who are always afraid they may go short. The Spaniard believed him or pretended to believe him, and, his eyes fixed on the horizon at the end of the road, thrummed and tormented his inseparable and companionable instrument. Paganini walked along on the other side of the road. It was a mutual convention, designed so they wouldn't get in each other's way. Thus both of them could practise, working as they walked along.

Then, when they reached a place which offered some chance of making a bit of money, one of the two would play one of his compositions, and the other would improvise, at his side, a variation, an accompaniment, a bass. The sheer enjoyment and poetry of this troubadour life of theirs no one will ever know. They separated, I don't know why. The

Spaniard continued his journey alone. One evening, he arrived in a small town in the Jura; he had bills posted and announced a concert in a room in the town hall. The concert was him, just him and his guitar. He had attracted attention by strumming away in a few cafés, and there were some musicians in town who had been struck by his strange talent. Well, a lot of people came along.

My Spaniard had unearthed, in a corner of town next to the cemetery, another Spaniard, someone from back home. This man was a kind of builder of burial places, a mason who constructed marble tombs. Like all those who have funereal trades, he liked a drink. So the bottle, and their shared fatherland, helped them along; musician and mason became inseparable. The very day of the concert, when the appointed hour came, they were together, but where? Nobody knew. They scoured all the taverns in the town, all the cafés. Finally he was unearthed with his friend, in an indescribably sleazy bar, completely drunk, as was the other. There followed scenes like those played by Kean and Frédérick[8]. Finally he agreed to go and play; but he was struck by a sudden idea: 'You'll play with me,' the Spaniard said to his friend. The latter refused; he did have a violin, but he played it as badly as the worst of fiddlers. 'You'll play, or else I won't.'

None of his friend's sermonising, none of his sensible objections were of any avail, and he had to give in. So there they were on the podium, standing in front of the elegant bourgeoisie of the place. 'Bring some wine,' said the Spaniard. The funeral mason, who was known to everybody, but to none as a musician, was too drunk to be in the least self-conscious. When the wine was brought, they were too impatient to bother uncorking the bottles. That rascally pair guillotined them with their knives, like people who haven't been brought up very well. Imagine what an effect this had on a provincial audience in all its finery! The ladies got up and left, and faced with these two drunkards who appeared half stupid, many people walked out, scandalised.

But it was all the better for those whose curiosity was not stifled by their sense of propriety and who had the strength of mind to stay. 'Begin,' said the guitarist to the mason. It is impossible to say what kind of sounds emerged from the drunken violin; Bacchus in delirium cutting stone with a saw. What did he play, what did he try to play? It doesn't matter much, the first tune he thought of. All at once, a sweet, lively, capricious melody, enveloped, drowned out, extinguished, and disguised the noisy uproar. The guitar sang so loud that the violin could no longer be heard. And yet it was the same tune, the wine-sodden tune that the mason had struck up.

The guitar expressed itself with immense sonority; it chattered, it sang, it declaimed with frightful verve, and with an unprecedented sureness and purity of diction. The guitar improvised a variation on the theme of the blind man's violin. It took its cue from it, and it dressed in splendid, maternal clothes the reedy nakedness of its sounds. My reader will understand how indescribable it is; a trustworthy and sober eyewitness told me what happened. At the end, the public was even more drunk than he was. The Spaniard was fêted, complimented, hailed with a tremendous outpouring of enthusiasm. But doubtless the character of the locals displeased him; for this was the only time he agreed to play.

And where is he now? Which sun gazed down on his last dreams? Which soil received his cosmopolitan remains? Which ditch sheltered his final agony? Where are the intoxicating perfumes of dead-and-gone flowers? Where are the fairy-tale colours of the sunsets of yesteryear?

3

I probably haven't told you anything really new. Everyone is familiar with wine; everyone loves it. When there is a real philosophical doctor, something you hardly ever find, he will be able to carry out a penetrating study of wine, a sort of twofold psychology, the two terms of which are wine and man. He will explain how and why certain drinks possess the ability of increasing immeasurably the personality of the thinking being, and of creating, so to speak, a third person – a mystical operation in which natural man and wine, the animal god and the vegetable god, play the roles of the Father and the Son in the Trinity; they engender a Holy Spirit who is the superior man who proceeds equally from the two of them.

There are people for whom wine's capacity to get their circulation flowing again is so great that their legs become firmer and their hearing excessively acute. I knew an individual whose weakened eyes found in drunkenness all their original piercing strength. Wine changed the mole into an eagle.

An old unknown author said, 'Nothing equals the joy of the man drinking, if not the joy of the wine at being drunk'. Indeed, wine plays an intimate role in the life of humanity, so intimate that I wouldn't be surprised if, seduced by pantheistic ideas, several reasonable characters were to ascribe to it a kind of personality. Wine and man make me think of two friendly wrestlers ever fighting and ever making up. The loser always embraces the victor.

There are wicked drunkards; they are people who are naturally wicked. The wicked man becomes abominable, just as the good man becomes truly excellent.

I will shortly be talking about a substance that has become

fashionable over the last few years, a sort of delightful drug for a certain category of dilettantish souls, the effects of which are far more overwhelming and potent than those of wine. I will carefully describe all its effects, then, resuming the depiction of the different ways in which wine is effective, I will compare these two artificial means with which man, by exacerbating his personality, creates so to speak a sort of divinity within himself.

I will demonstrate the drawbacks of hashish, the least of which – despite the unknown store of benevolence it apparently brings out in man's heart, or rather brain – the least defect, I say, is that of being antisocial, while wine is profoundly humane and, I would almost go so far as to say, comparable to a man of action.

4

HASHISH

When hemp is harvested, strange phenomena sometimes occur in the bodies of the male and female labourers. You'd say that there was, rising from the harvest, some mysterious, vertigo-inducing spirit spiralling up their legs and maliciously climbing up to their brain. The harvester's head is set swirling; at other times it is made heavy with reverie. His limbs grow weak and refuse to carry out their tasks. Furthermore, I too, when I was a child, romping and rolling in heaps of lucerne, experienced analogous phenomena.

People have tried to make hashish with hemp from France. All efforts up until now have failed, and the fanatics who want to procure magical pleasures for themselves at any price have continued to use hashish that has crossed the Mediterranean, in other words, that is made from Indian or Egyptian hemp.

Hashish is composed of a decoction of Indian hemp, butter and a small quantity of opium.

You have a green jelly, with a strangely powerful smell, so powerful that it arouses a certain revulsion, as, indeed, would any fine odour intensified to its maximum strength and, so to speak, density. Take an amount as big as a nutshell, fill a small spoon with it, and happiness is yours; absolute happiness with all its intoxication, all its youthful follies, and all its infinite beatitude. There lies happiness, in the form of a small lump of jelly; take it without fear, it won't kill you; your physical organs are not in the least bit seriously damaged by it. Perhaps your will-power will be lessened by it, but that's another matter.

Generally to bring out all the strength of hashish and give it its full effect, you have to dilute it in very hot black coffee, and take it on an empty stomach; dinner must be postponed until ten or twelve o'clock at night; a very light soup is all that is allowed. An infraction to this simplest of rules would lead either to vomiting, due to the dinner not agreeing with the drug, or to the hashish not being effective. Many ignorant or idiotic people who behave like this accuse hashish of being powerless.

Hardly has the little drug been absorbed – an operation which does actually require a certain resolve, for as I have said, the mixture smells so strong that it makes some people feel quite nauseous – than you immediately find yourself in a state of anxiety. You have vaguely heard of the wonderful effects of hashish, your imagination has conjured up a particular idea, an ideal of intoxication, and you are longing to know if the reality, if the result will live up to your preconception. The time that elapses between the absorption of the potion and the first symptoms varies with temperament and also with habit. Experienced hashish-takers sometimes feel the first symptoms of the invasion after half an hour.

I forgot to say that as hashish causes in man an exacerbation of his personality as well as a very vivid sense of his circumstances and environment, it is best to submit to its effects only in favourable environments and circumstances. Every joy, every sense of well-being is superabundant, and likewise every pain, every anguish is deep and intense. Do not perform such an experiment on yourself if you have a bothersome piece of business to transact, if your mind is inclined to spleen, or if you have a bill to pay. I've already told you, hashish is unsuited to action. It does not console like wine; it merely develops the human personality to an immeasurable degree in the current circumstances in which it is placed. As far as possible, you need a fine apartment or a fine landscape, a carefree and detached mind, a few accomplices whose intellectual temperament is close to yours, and a little music too, if possible.

Most of the time, novices, on their first initiation, complain of the slowness of the effects. They await them anxiously, and as things don't move fast enough for their liking, they start to boast at their incredulity, which causes much merriment among those who know what's what and the way hashish has to be handled. It is not the least comical of things to see the first effects take hold and develop in the very midst of this incredulity. At first a certain weird and irresistible hilarity takes hold of you. The commonest words, the simplest ideas assume a bizarre new appearance. This gaiety strikes you yourself as intolerable; but it is useless to jib. The demon has invaded you; all the efforts you make to resist will only help to accelerate the progress of the sickness. You laugh at your silliness and your madness; your comrades laugh in your face, and you feel no resentment, for feelings of benevolence are starting to spread.

This languid gaiety, this sense of queasiness in joy, this insecurity, this sickly hesitancy generally last only a short while. Soon the associations of ideas become so vague, the threads that link your conceptions so tenuous, that your accomplices, your fellow celebrants are the only ones who can understand you. Your frolics, your fits of laughter seem the height of stupidity to any man who is not in the same state as you.

The sensible caution of this unhappy man increases your merriment immeasurably, his cool detachment pushes you to the uttermost limits of irony; he seems to you the craziest and most ridiculous of all men. As for your comrades, you can understand them perfectly well. Soon you understand each other simply through your glances. In fact it's a somewhat comical situation, that of men enjoying a gaiety incomprehensible to anyone not situated in the same world as they are. They feel a sense of profound pity for such a man. From that moment, the idea of your own superiority starts to dawn on the horizon of your intellect. Soon it will grow to huge dimensions.

I have witnessed, in this first phase, two rather grotesque scenes. A famous musician who was unaware of the properties of hashish, and perhaps had never heard of them, arrived at a gathering where almost everybody had taken some. They tried to get him to understand its marvellous effects. He laughed graciously, like a man who is happy to adopt a pose for a few minutes out of a sense of propriety, because he is well brought up. They laughed uproariously; for the man who has taken hashish is, in the first phase, endowed with a marvellous sense of the comic. The fits of laughter, the incomprehensible and outrageous nonsense, the inextricable plays on words, the baroque gestures continued. The musician declared that this artistic overacting was a bad thing, and that moreover it must be really tiring for the performers.

The merriment increased. 'This overacting is perhaps good for you, but not for me,' he said. 'So long as it's good for us,' replied one of the sick men selfishly. Endless fits of laughter filled the room. My hero got angry and wanted to leave. Someone locked the door and hid the key. Another fell to his knees before him, and declared to him in tears, in the name of all those present, that while they were moved on his behalf and filled with the deepest pity for his inferiority, they were nonetheless prompted by feelings of eternal benevolence.

They begged him to play some music, he accepted resignedly. Hardly had the violin struck up a tune than the sounds that spread through the apartment took hold of one or other of the sick men. The room was filled with deep sighs, sobs, heart-rending groans, floods of tears. The horrified musician stopped, thinking he must be in an asylum. He went up to the one whose bliss was expressing itself most noisily; he asked him if he was in great pain and what would help to relieve it. A positivist spirit, who had also abstained from tasting the beatific drug, suggested lemonade and acids. The sick man, his eyes gleaming ecstatically, looked at him with unspeakable contempt; only his pride restrained him from uttering the most withering insults. And indeed, what is more likely to exasperate someone filled with a crazy joy than an attempt to try and cure him?

Here, in my opinion, is an extremely curious phenomenon: a servant girl, requested to bring tobacco and refreshments to people under the influence of hashish, seeing herself surrounded by weird facial expressions, eyes popping out of heads, and, so to speak, circumscribed on all sides by an unhealthy atmosphere, by this collective madness, uttered a shrill, senseless laugh, dropped the tray, which shattered together with all the cups and glasses on it, and fled in terror as fast as her legs would carry her. Everyone laughed. She admitted the following day that she had felt something strange for several hours, she had 'come over all queer, I just can't describe it'. And yet she hadn't taken any hashish.

The second phase is heralded by a sensation of chilliness in the extremities, a great weakness; you have, as they say, butter-fingers, your head feels heavy and a general sluggishness creeps over your body. Your eyes bulge more and more, they are as it were pulled in every direction by an implacable ecstasy. Your face is suffused by pallor, it becomes livid and greenish of hue. Your lips become thin and pinched and seem to want to disappear back into your face. Deep, raucous sighs emerge from your breast, as if your previous nature could not stand the weight of your new one. Your senses become extraordinarily fine and acute. Your eyes can pierce the infinite. Your ears can perceive the most imperceptible sounds even amid the loudest din.

The hallucinations begin. External objects take on monstrous appearances. They reveal themselves to you in shapes hitherto unknown. Then they become deformed, transformed, and finally they enter into your very being, or you enter into them. The strangest equivocations, the most inexplicable transpositions of ideas take place. Sounds have their own colour, colours make music. Musical notes are numbers, and you can perform with frightening rapidity astounding arithmetic calculations as the music uncoils in your ears. You are sitting down, smoking; you think you are sitting in your pipe, and it's you that your pipe is smoking; it's you that you are breathing out in the form of blue tinged clouds.

You are feeling perfectly comfortable, only one thing is

bothering you and causing you some anxiety. How will you be able to get out of your pipe? You mull over this for a whole eternity. An interval of lucidity enables you with a great effort to look at the clock. Eternity has lasted a minute. Another stream of ideas sweeps you away; it will sweep you away in its living whirlpool for a minute, and this minute will be yet another eternity. The proportions of time and being are distorted by the innumerable multitude and intensity of sensations and ideas. You live several human lives in the space of an hour. This is the subject of *The Wild Ass's Skin*[9]. There is no longer any correspondence between your organs and the intense pleasures they feel.

From time to time your personality disappears. The objectivity that makes certain poets pantheists and produces great actors becomes so profound that you merge with external beings. You are turned into a tree soughing in the wind and spinning out vegetable melodies to nature. Now you are hovering in the azure heights of an immensely vaster sky. All pain has disappeared. You are no longer struggling, you are carried away, you are no longer master of yourself and you are not in the least bothered by this. Before long the idea of time will completely vanish. From time to time a short period of awakening still intervenes. It seems to you that you are emerging from a wonderful, fantastic world. True, you continue to possess the capacity to observe yourself, and tomorrow you will still be able to remember some of your sensations. But this psychological faculty is one you can no longer apply. I defy you to sharpen a quill or a pencil; it would be a labour beyond your strength.

At other times music narrates infinite poems to you, sets you amidst frightening or magical dramas. It becomes associated with objects right under your eyes. The paintings on the ceiling, even if they are mediocre or downright bad, are endowed with a startling vividness. Limpid, bewitching water flows through the tremulous grass. Nymphs with bright, gleaming flesh gaze at you with wide eyes more limpid than the water and the azure sky. You could take your place and play your role in the least attractive paintings, or the coarsest wallpaper on tavern walls.

I have noticed that water assumes an alarming seductiveness for all artistically inclined minds when they are illuminated by hashish. Flowing water, fountains, rippling cascades, the blue immensity of the sea, roll along, sleeping and singing in the depths of your mind. It might perhaps not be a good idea to leave a man in this state next to a stretch of limpid water; like the fisherman in the ballad, he might perhaps allow himself to be dragged down by Undine.

Towards the end of the evening, you can eat, but this operation is not performed without difficulty. You find yourself so elevated above material facts that you would certainly prefer to remain stretched out at full length in the depths of your intellectual paradise. Sometimes however your appetite increases to an extraordinary degree; but you need enormous will-power to handle a bottle, a fork and a knife.

The third phase, separated from the second by a renewed crisis, a dizzying bout of intoxication followed by a new sense of queasiness, is something indescribable. It is what Orientals call 'kief'; it is absolute bliss. It is no longer something swirling and tumultuous. It is a calm and immobile bliss. All philosophical problems are solved. All the arduous questions which theologians have ever skirmished with, and which are the despair of humanity when it tries to reason, have now become limpid and clear. All contradiction has become unity. Man has qualified as God.

There is something in you which says: 'You are superior to all men, no one understands what you are thinking, what you are feeling now. They are even incapable of understanding the immense love you feel for them. But you mustn't hate them for that; you must pity them. A vast expanse of happiness and virtue is opening up before you. No one will ever know the degree of virtue and intelligence that you have attained. Live in the solitude of your thought, and make sure you do not inflict pain on mankind.'

One of the most grotesque effects of hashish is the fear, so great as to be an obsessive phobia, of inflicting pain on anyone. You would even, if you had the strength, disguise the extra-natural state which you are in, so as not to cause anxiety to the least of men.

In this supreme state, love, in tender and artistic minds, assumes the strangest forms and lends itself to the most baroque schemes. An unbridled libertinage can be mingled with a feeling of ardent and affectionate paternity.

The last observation I have to make is no less curious. When, the following morning, you see daylight flooding into your room, your first sensation is profound astonishment. Time had completely disappeared. Just now it was night-time, now it's daytime. 'Did I sleep, or didn't I sleep? Did my intoxication last all night, and, as all notion of time was suppressed, did the whole night barely seem to last a second for me? Or was I enshrouded in the folds of vision-filled sleep?' It is impossible to know.

It seems to you that you are experiencing a sense of well-being and a wonderful lightness of spirit; no tiredness. But no sooner have you got up than an old trace of your previous intoxicated state becomes apparent. Your tottering legs carry you cautiously along, you are frightened that you might break like some fragile object. A profound languor, not without its charm, overwhelms your mind. You are incapable of working and lack the energy for action.

This is the deserved punishment for the impious prodigality with which you have spent such a great quantity of nervous fluid. You have cast your personality to the four winds of heaven, and now you find it hard to put it together again and focus it.

5

I'm not saying that hashish produces on all men all the effects I have just described. I have narrated more or less the phenomena which are generally produced, with a few variants, in artistic and philosophical minds. But there are temperaments in whom this drug merely brings out a crazed rowdiness, a violent gaiety that resembles giddiness, dancing, hopping, stamping, fits of laughter. They have, so to speak, an altogether material hashish. They are intolerable in the eyes of spiritualists who feel great pity for them. Their nasty personality shows up clearly. I once saw a respectable magistrate, an honourable man, as those in high society say of themselves, one of those men whose artificial solemnity always creates an imposing impression who, the minute hashish invaded him, started to dance the most indecent cancan you could possibly imagine. The inner, authentic monster thus revealed itself. This man who sat in judgement on the actions of his fellow men, this *Togatus*, had learnt the cancan in secret.

So it can be deduced that the impersonality and objectivity that I have mentioned, and that is merely the excessive development of the poetic spirit, will never be found in the hashish of men like that.

6

In Egypt, the government bans the buying and trafficking of hashish, at least inside the country. The unfortunate souls in prey to this passion come to the chemist's to pick up, on the pretext of purchasing another drug, their small pre-prepared dose. The Egyptian government is quite right. Never could a reasonable state subsist if hashish could be freely used. It produces neither warriors nor citizens. Indeed, it is forbidden to man, on pain of degradation and intellectual death, to disturb the primordial conditions of his existence, and to destroy the equilibrium between his faculties and their environments. If there were a government intent on corrupting its subjects, it would need merely to encourage the use of hashish.

They say this substance causes no physical harm. That's true, at least up until now. For I don't know to what extent you can call a man who spends all his time dreaming and is incapable of action 'healthy', even if all his limbs are in good shape. But it is the will that is attacked, and this is our most precious organ. Never will a man who can, with a spoonful of jelly, procure for himself instantaneously all that heaven and earth can offer, deign to work in order to acquire the thousandth part of it. But before all else we must live and work.

I had the idea of talking about wine and hashish in the same article because there is indeed a common element they share: they develop to an excessive degree man's poetic character. Man's frenzied love of all substances, whether healthy or dangerous, which exalt his personality, bears witness to his greatness. He is always aspiring to rekindle his hopes and to rise up to the infinite. But you need to look at the results. Here is a liquor that activates the digestion, fortifies the muscles, and enriches the blood. Even when taken in great quantities, it causes only relatively short-lived disorders. Here is a substance that interrupts the digestive functions, weakens the limbs and can cause an intoxication lasting for twenty-four hours. Wine elevates the will, hashish annihilates it. Wine is a physical aid, hashish a weapon for the suicidal. Wine makes one good and outgoing. Hashish is isolating. One is hard-working, so to speak, the other is essentially idle. What indeed is the point of working, ploughing, writing, producing anything at all, when you can gain paradise at a stroke? Finally wine is for the ordinary people who work hard and deserve to drink it. Hashish belongs to the class of solitary joys; it is made for wretched idlers. Wine is useful, it produces results that will bear fruit. Hashish is useless and dangerous.*

7

I'll finish this article with a few fine words which are not by me, but by a remarkable and little-known philosopher, Barbereau, a musical theorist and professor at the conservatoire. I was with him at a gathering where several people had partaken of the bliss-inducing poison, and he said to me in tones of unspeakable contempt: 'I can't understand why rational and spiritual man uses artificial means to attain poetic bliss, since enthusiasm and will-power are sufficient to

---

* Just for the record, the attempt made recently to apply hashish to the treatment of madness should be mentioned. The madman who takes hashish contracts a new madness which drives out the other one, and when the intoxication has passed, real madness, which is the normal state of the madman, resumes its sway, as reason and good health do in us. Someone has taken the trouble to write a book about it. The doctor who has invented this system isn't in the least bit a philosopher. [10]

elevate him to a supernatural existence. The great poets, the philosophers, the prophets are beings who by the pure and free exercise of their will reach a state in which they are at once cause and effect, subject and object, hypnotist and sleepwalker.'

I think exactly as he does.

1. Jean-Anthelme Brillat-Savarin (1755–1826) was a French gastronomist (and magistrate). His *Physiologie du goût* (1825) did indeed have little to say on wine (though slightly more than Baudelaire credits him with), but its comments on food and the art of living made it eminently quotable.

2. Johann Caspar Lavater (1741–1801) was a Swiss writer: Baudelaire may have been quoting from a work of his translated into French in 1805, entitled *Lavater's Last Gift To His Friends*.

3. François Béroalde de Verville (1556–*c*.1629) was an encyclopedic writer on love, science, ethics, theology, and metaphysics: *Le Moyen de parvenir* (*How To Succeed*, 1610) is a satirical dialogue.

4. *Kreisleriana* by E.T.A. Hoffmann (1776–1822) are humorous essays and stories based on the life of the fictitious Kappelmeister Johannes Kreisler.

5. The 'number seven' was a phrase for the hook used by rag-pickers in their scavenging.

6. The River Pactolus in Lydia was famous in ancient times for the particles of gold it swept along in its sand.

7. Martin Drolling (1752–1827) was a painter whose *Kitchen Interior* is in the Louvre. Baudelaire may here be referring to the painter Jean-Louis-Ernest Meissonier (1815–91), a genre painter whom he knew personally.

8. Edmund Kean (1787/90–1833) was a great tragic (especially Shakespearean) actor; Frédérick Lemaître (1800–76), an emotional and virtuosic French Romantic actor (one of his performances was in fact as Kean, in the play of that name by Dumas *père*, 1836). Kean was prone to drunkenness.

9. *The Wild Ass's Skin* (*La Peau de Chagrin*) by Balzac is a novella whose basic topic is how to make the maximum use of one's finite time and energy. The hero, Raphaël, comes into possession of a wild ass' skin that grants its owner's wishes, but shrinks each time it is used for this purpose.

10. Dr Moreau de Tours is a doctor whose book *Du Hachisch et de l'aliénation mentale* (*On Hashish and Madness*) was published in 1845.

The Poem of Hashish

1

THE TASTE FOR THE INFINITE

Those who are capable of observing themselves, and retain the memory of their impressions, those who have been able, like Hoffmann, to construct their own spiritual barometer, have sometimes noticed, from the observatory of their minds, seasons of fine weather, days of happiness, and minutes of delight. There are days on which man wakes up feeling a young and vigorous mental power. Hardly has he wiped from his eyes the sleep that had sealed them, than the external world presents itself to him with striking vividness, sharpness of outline, and a wealth of admirable colours. The spiritual world opens up vast perspectives, full of brilliant new possibilities. Gratified by this bliss, which is unfortunately rare and transient, man feels at once more artistic and, in short, more just and more noble. But the strangest thing about this exceptional state of mind and senses, which I can without exaggeration call paradisiacal, if I compare it with the oppressive darkness of common, day-to-day existence, is that it has been produced by no clearly visible or easily definable cause. Is it the result of proper hygiene and a sensible lifestyle? This is the first explanation that comes to mind; but we are obliged to acknowledge that often this marvel, this near-miracle, is produced as if it were the effect of a higher, invisible power, external to man, following a period in which the latter has been abusing his physical faculties. Are we to say that it is the recompense for assiduous prayer and spiritual fervour? It is certain that a constant elevation of desire, a heavenwards inclination of one's spiritual forces, would be the lifestyle most apt to create this mental health, so radiant and glorious; but by virtue of what absurd law does it sometimes manifest itself following guilty orgies of the imagination, after a sophistical use of reason, which bears the same relation to its decent, sensible use as do contortionists' tricks to healthy gymnastics? This is why I prefer to consider this abnormal condition of the mind as a real gift of grace, as a magic mirror in which man is invited to see himself at his most attractive, in other words as he should be and could be; a kind of angelic stimulus, a call to order of a flattering kind. In the same way, a certain spiritualist school, which has its representatives in England and America, considers supernatural phenomena such as the apparitions of phantoms, ghosts, etc., to be manifestations of the divine will, intent on reawakening in man's mind the memory of invisible realities.

Furthermore, this strange, captivating state, in which all one's forces are in a condition of equilibrium, in which the imagination, although marvellously powerful, does not drag the moral sense after it on perilous adventures, in which an exquisite sensibility is no longer tormented by unhealthy nerves, which so often impel one to crime or despair, this marvellous state, I say, comes with no warning symptoms. It is as unexpected as a phantom. It is a certain haunting feeling, albeit an intermittent one, from which we should deduce, if we were wise, the certainty of a better existence and the hope of reaching it through the daily exercise of our will. This acuteness of thought, this enthusiasm of the senses and the spirit, must, at all times, have appeared to man to be the greatest good; that is why, considering only his immediate pleasures, and without worrying that he might be violating the laws of his constitution, he has sought in physical science, in pharmaceutics, in the grossest liquors, in the most subtle perfumes, in every climate and at every period of history, the means of escaping, if only for a few hours, his dwelling-place in the mire and, as the author of *Lazare* puts it, tried 'to capture paradise at a single blow'.[1] Alas! man's vices, however horrifying they are said to be, contain the proof (even if only in their infinite capacity for expansion!) of his taste for the infinite; but it is a taste which often takes the wrong path. We could apply in a metaphorical sense the commonplace proverb 'All roads lead to Rome' to the moral world; all roads lead to reward or punishment, two forms of eternity. The human spirit is brimming over with passions; it has enough and to spare, to use another trivial turn of speech; but this unhappy spirit, whose natural depravation is just as great as its sudden and almost paradoxical aptitude for charity and the most arduous of virtues, is fertile in paradoxes which allow it to employ in the service of evil the excess of this overflowing passion. The human spirit never believes it is selling itself wholesale. It forgets, in its infatuation, that it is playing against a subtler and stronger spirit than itself, and that the Spirit of Evil, should you allow it merely to get hold of a single hair, will soon carry off the entire head. This visible lord of visible nature (man, that is) has tried to capture paradise at a single blow, by fermented drinks, and he is thus like a maniac replacing solid furniture and real gardens by stage-sets painted on canvas and mounted on frames. It is in this perversion of the sense of the infinite that lies, in my opinion, the reason behind every culpable excess, from the solitary and concentrated intoxication of the man of letters who, obliged to seek in opium a relief for his physical pain, and having thereby discovered a source of intense and morbid pleasures, has little by little turned it into his unique regimen and, as it were, the sun of his spiritual life, to the most repellent drunkenness of the poorer parts of town, where its victims, brains afire with dreams of glory, wallow ridiculously in the filth of the street.

Among the drugs best able to produce what I call the *Artificial Ideal*, apart from liquor (which soon leads its drinkers to real bodily fury and lays prostrate their spiritual strength) and perfumes (the excessive use of which, while making man's imagination more subtle, gradually drains his physical strength), the two most potent substances, those most convenient to use and most ready to hand, are hashish and opium. The analysis of the mysterious effects and the morbid pleasures that these drugs can produce, of the inevitable retribution that results from their prolonged use, and finally of the very immorality implied in this pursuit of a false ideal, constitutes the subject of this study.

An investigation into opium has already been carried out, and in such a brilliant way, medical and poetic at once, that I would not dare add anything to it. So I will content myself, in another study, with presenting an analysis of that incomparable book, which has never been completely translated in France. The author, an illustrious man of powerful and exquisite imagination, living today in seclusion and silence, had the courage, and the tragic honesty, to narrate the pleasures and the tortures that he once found in opium, and the most dramatic part of his book is where he talks about the superhuman efforts of will-power he had to deploy in order to escape the damnation to which he had rashly doomed himself.

Today, I will be talking just about hashish, and I will be talking about it on the basis of extensive and detailed evidence, extracted from notes or remarks made by intelligent men who had long been addicts. But I will meld these varied documents into a sort of monograph, choosing as an example a single soul, one that is easy to explain and define, as the type most prone to experiences of this nature.

2
WHAT IS HASHISH?

The narratives of Marco Polo, which have been unjustly mocked, like those of several other travellers of olden days, have been verified by scholars and deserve our credence. I will not repeat his story of how the Old Man of the Mountain, having first intoxicated them with hashish (whence Hashishins or Assassins), locked up, in a garden full of delights, those of his youngest disciples to whom he wished to give an idea of paradise, as a glimpse, so to speak, of the reward they would earn for their passive and unreflecting obedience. The reader can consult, on the secret society of the Hashishins, the book by Herr von Hammer and the memorandum by M. Sylvestre de Sacy, contained in volume XVI of the *Mémoires de l'Académie des Inscriptions et Belles-Lettres*, and, on the etymology of the word *assassin*, his letter to the editor of the *Moniteur*, included in issue 359 (1809).[2] Herodotus tells how the Scythians would gather hempseeds onto which they threw red-hot stones. For them it was like a steam bath more strongly scented than the steam of any Greek hot-room, and the pleasure they derived from it was so intense that it drew from them cries of joy.

Hashish does indeed come to us from the Orient; the stimulant properties of hemp were well-known in Ancient Egypt, and it is widely used, under different names, in India, in Algeria, and in Arabia Felix. But we have, closer to home, under our very eyes in fact, curious examples of intoxication caused by vegetable emanations. Leaving aside the children who, having romped and rolled in piles of mown lucerne, often experience strange attacks of giddiness, it is well-known that when hemp is harvested, the male and female labourers suffer similar effects; it is as if there arose a miasma from the harvest, leading to malignant disturbances in their brains. The harvester's head seems to swirl violently, and sometimes grows heavy and dreamy. At certain moments, a weakness spreads through the limbs that refuse to carry out their tasks. We have heard of not infrequent bouts of sleepwalking among Russian peasants, which must, it is said, be ascribed to the use of hempseed oil in the preparation of their food. Who has not come across the extravagant behaviour of hens that have been pecking up hempseeds, and the impetuous enthusiasm of the horses which peasants, at weddings and on feast-days of their parish saints, train for a steeplechase by feeding them a ration of hempseed, sometimes mixed with a little wine?

However, French hemp is unsuitable for making hashish, or at least, as repeated experiments have shown, unsuitable for producing a drug that equals hashish in potency. Hashish, or Indian hemp, *cannabis indica*, is a plant from the family of Urticaceae, similar in every respect to the hemp of our climates, apart from the fact that it doesn't grow to the same height. It possesses the most intoxicating properties which, for several years, have been attracting in France the attention of scientists and people in polite society. It is more or less highly esteemed depending on its different places of origin; the hemp of Bengal is that most prized by devotees; but those of Egypt, Constantinople, Persia and Algeria possess the same properties, although to a lesser degree.

Hashish (or grass, that is to say *the* grass par excellence, as if the Arabs had wanted to define in one word *grass* the source of all immaterial pleasures) comes under different names, depending on its composition and the kind of preparation it has undergone in the country where it was harvested: in India, *bhang*; in Africa, *teriaki*; in Algeria and Yemen, *madjound*, etc.

The season of the year in which it is gathered is a matter of some importance; it is when it is in flower that it possesses its greatest potency; the flowering tops are consequently the only parts employed in the different preparations, which we shall now say a few words about.

The fatty extract of hashish, as the Arabs prepare it, is obtained by boiling the tops of the fresh plant in butter with a little water. You filter it after the complete evaporation of all the liquid, and you thereby obtain a preparation that has the appearance of an ointment of yellowish-green colour, which retains a disagreeable odour of hashish and rancid butter. In this form, it is used in little pellets of two to four grams; but because of its repellent smell, which increases with time, the Arabs make the fatty extract into a kind of jelly.

The most commonly used of these jellies, *dawamesk*, is a mixture of fatty extract, sugar and various herbs and spices, such as vanilla, cinnamon, pistachios, almonds, and musk. Sometimes they even add a little cantharides, to produce an effect that has nothing in common with that usually brought about by hashish. In this new form, there is nothing unpleasant about hashish, and you can take it in doses of fifteen, twenty and thirty grams, either sandwiched by a slice of wafer, or in a cup of coffee.

The experiments carried out by Messrs Smith, Gastinel and Decourtive were designed to discover the active principle of hashish. Despite their efforts, its chemical composition is still little known; but its properties are generally ascribed to a resinous matter found in it in quite large doses, in a proportion of roughly ten per cent. To obtain this resin, you reduce the dried plant to a coarse powder, washing it several times in alcohol that you then distil so as partly to eliminate it; you evaporate it to the consistency of an extract; you treat this extract with water, which dissolves the gummy foreign matter, and the resin is then left in a pure state.

This product is soft, dark green in colour, and possesses to a high degree the characteristic odour of hashish. Five, ten, or fifteen centigrams are enough to produce surprising effects. But hashish, which can be administered in the form of chocolate lozenges or small ginger-flavoured pills, has – as do *dawamesk* and the fatty extract – effects of greater or lesser potency, varying greatly with the temperament of different individuals and their nervous susceptibility. What is more, the result can vary in one and the same individual. Sometimes it involves an immoderate and irresistible gaiety, sometimes a feeling of well-being and plenitude of life, at other times an ambiguous slumber shot through with dreams. There are, however, phenomena which are reproduced quite regularly, especially in people of comparable temperament and education; there is a kind of unity in variety that will enable me to compose without too much difficulty the monograph on intoxication which I mentioned just now.

In Constantinople, in Algeria, and even in France, some people smoke hashish mixed with tobacco, but then the phenomena in question are produced only in a very moderate and, so to speak, sluggish form. I have heard that recently, by distillation, an essential oil had been derived from hashish which appears to possess a much more active virtue than all preparations known hitherto; but it has not been studied sufficiently for me to speak with any certainty of its results. It is no doubt superfluous to add that tea, coffee and liqueurs are powerful aids which accelerate to a greater or lesser degree the full development of this mysterious intoxication.

'What do you feel? What do you see? Marvellous things, I suppose? Extraordinary sights? Is it really beautiful? and really terrible? and really dangerous?' – These are among the ordinary questions addressed, with a mixture of curiosity and fear, by the ignorant to the proficient. They seem to have a childish impatience for knowledge, like people who have never left their own hearths when they find themselves face to face with a man returning from far-away, unknown places. They imagine the intoxication of hashish to be like a wonderful country, a vast theatre of conjuring tricks and vanishing acts, where everything is miraculous and unexpected. This is a false notion, a complete misapprehension. And since, for the common run of readers and questioners the word hashish involves the idea of a strange, topsy-turvy world, and the expectation of wonderful dreams (it would be better to call them hallucinations, which are in fact less frequent than they are supposed to be), I must immediately point out the significant difference that distinguishes the effects of hashish from the phenomena of sleep. In sleep, that adventure-filled journey we make every night, there is something positively miraculous; it is a miracle whose mystery has been blunted by its regular recurrence. Man's dreams are of two classes. The first kind, filled with the details of his ordinary life, his preoccupations, his desires, and his vices, combine more or less bizarrely with objects seen in the daytime, which have indiscreetly fixed themselves on the vast canvas of his memory. This is natural dreaming; it is the man himself. But as for the other kind of dream! the absurd, unexpected dream, unrelated and unconnected to the sleeper's character, life, and passions!

This dream, which I will call hieroglyphical, obviously represents the supernatural side of man, and it is precisely because it is absurd that the Ancients thought it divine. As it is inexplicable by natural causes, they decided its cause lay outside man; and even today, interpreters of dreams notwithstanding, there is a philosophical school which sees in dreams of this kind sometimes a reproach, sometimes a piece of advice; in short, a symbolic mental picture, produced in the very mind of the sleeper. It is a dictionary which must be studied, a language to which wise men can obtain the key.

In the intoxication of hashish, there is nothing of the sort. We never emerge from natural dreaming. True, the intoxication, from beginning to end, is merely an immense dream, thanks to the intensity of its colours and the rapidity of its imaginings; but it always retains the tonality peculiar to the individual. Man has chosen to dream and his dreams will in turn govern him; but the dream will still be its father's son. The idler has done his utmost to introduce the supernatural into his life and his thought by artificial means; but he is merely, after all his efforts, and despite the incidental intensity of his sensations, the same man writ large, the same number raised to a very high power. He is subjugated; but, unfortunately for him, he is subjugated only by himself, in other words by the part of himself already predominant; *he wanted to be an angel, he has become a beast*[4], momentarily a very powerful beast, if indeed one can apply the word 'power' to an excessive sensibility ungoverned by any force able to moderate it or make use of it.

So the people in polite society and the ignorant, curious to experience exceptionally intense pleasures, should know that they will find in hashish nothing miraculous, absolutely nothing other than what is excessively natural. The brain and the organism on which hashish operates will merely produce their ordinary, individual phenomena, increased, it is true, in quality and intensity, but always faithful to their origin. Man will not escape the fatal thrall of his physical and mental temperament: hashish will be, for a man's familiar impressions and thoughts, a magnifying mirror, but still just a mirror.

Look at the drug lying in front of you: a bit of green jelly, the size of a nut, with a strangely powerful smell, so powerful that it arouses a certain revulsion and a desire to be sick, as indeed would any fine and even pleasant odour intensified to its maximum strength and, so to speak, density. Let me, in passing, point out that this proposition can be taken vice versa, and that the most repellent, most revolting odour would perhaps become pleasurable if it were reduced to its smallest quantity and power of diffusion. – Here then is happiness! In volume it is as much as a teaspoon can hold! Happiness with all its intoxication, all its follies, all its puerility. You can swallow it without fear; it won't kill you. Your physical organs will not be in the least bit damaged by it. Later, perhaps, over-frequent resort to the spell will diminish your will-power, perhaps you will be less of a man than you are today; but the retribution is so far-off, and the future disaster of a nature so difficult to determine! What do you risk? A little nervous fatigue tomorrow. Don't you risk every day greater punishment for lesser rewards? So that's that: you have even, to give it greater strength and expansion, diluted your dose of fatty extract in a cup of black coffee; you have taken care to keep your stomach empty, postponing your main meal until nine or ten o'clock in the evening, so as to leave the poison complete freedom to act; in an hour at most you will take some light soup. Now you are well enough ballasted for a long and strange journey. The steam-whistle has blown, the sails are set, and you have over ordinary travellers the curious advantage of not knowing where you are going. You asked for it; long live destiny!

I presume that you have taken the precaution of carefully choosing the right moment for this intrepid expedition. Every perfect debauch needs perfect leisure. Moreover, you know that hashish leads to an exaggeration not just of the individual involved, but also of his circumstances and surroundings; make sure you have no duties to perform which require punctuality or precision; no family worries; none of the pains of love. You have to be careful about this. A worry, an anxiety, a memory of some duty requiring the exercise of your will-power and your attention at a specific moment would come to toll like a knell through your intoxication, and poison your pleasure. The anxiety would become anguish; the worry, real torture. If all these preliminary conditions have been observed, if the weather is fine, if you find yourself in a favourable environment, like a picturesque landscape or a poetically decorated apartment, if furthermore you can count on a little music, then everything is for the best.

Generally in hashish intoxication there are three quite easily distinguishable phases, and it is rather curious to observe novices experiencing the first symptoms of the first phase. You have vaguely heard of the wonderful effects of hashish; your imagination has imagined in advance a particular idea, something like an ideal of intoxication; and you are longing to know if the reality really will live up to your expectation. This is enough for you to be thrown right from the start into a state of anxiety, quite favourable to the all-conquering, invasive mood of the poison. Most novices, on the first step of their initiation, complain of the slowness of the effect; they await it with puerile impatience, and, as the drug doesn't act fast enough for them, they indulge in boastful expressions of incredulity which cause much merriment among the old initiates who know how hashish has to be handled. The first effects, like the symptoms of a storm that has been slowly brewing for a long time, appear and multiply in the very midst of this incredulity. At first a certain weird and irresistible hilarity takes hold of you. These attacks of inexplicable gaiety, which you feel almost ashamed of, recur frequently, and interrupt intervals of stupor during which you try in vain to gather your wits. The simplest words, the most trivial ideas assume a bizarre new appearance; you are even surprised to have found them so simple before now. Incongruous resemblances and associations of ideas, quite impossible to foresee, interminable puns, attempts at comedy, spring continually from your brain. The demon has invaded you; it is useless to jib at this hilarity, which is as painful as someone tickling you. From time to time you laugh at yourself, at your silliness and your madness, and your comrades – if you have any – laugh both at your state and at their own; but, as they are without malice, you feel no resentment.

This gaiety, in turn languid or piercing, this sense of queasiness in joy, this insecurity, this sickly hesitancy generally lasts only a short while. Soon the associations of ideas become so vague, the thread linking your conceptions so tenuous, that only your partners in hashish can understand you. And even here, in this particular area, there is no means of verification; perhaps they think they can understand you, and the illusion is reciprocal. These frolics, these fits of laughter, which resemble explosions, appear to be a real madness, or at least the inanity of a maniac, to any man not in the same state as you are. Likewise, the rationality and common sense, the regular train of thought of the prudent onlooker who has not become intoxicated, cause you much merriment and amuse you like a particular kind of insanity. The roles have been reversed. His composure pushes you to the uttermost limits of irony. Is it not a mysteriously comical situation, that of a man enjoying a gaiety which is incomprehensible to anyone who has not participated in the same milieu? The madman pities the wise man, and from that moment the idea of his superiority starts to dawn on the horizon of his intellect. Soon it will grow bigger, swelling and bursting like a meteor.

I have been witness to a scene of this kind that went really quite far, and whose grotesque character was intelligible only to those acquainted, at least through observing others, with the effects of the substance and the enormous difference in range it produces between two intelligences supposed to be equal. A famous musician, who was unaware of the properties of hashish and perhaps had never heard of them, found himself at a gathering where several people had taken it. They tried to get him to understand its marvellous effects. On hearing these amazing stories, he smiled graciously, out of politeness, like a man who is happy to adopt a pose for a few minutes. His failure of understanding was soon guessed at by minds sharpened by the poison, and their laughter wounded him. Those outbursts of merriment, those puns, those strangely affected expressions, that whole unhealthy atmosphere irritated him and obliged him to declare, sooner perhaps than he might have wished, *that this artistic overacting was a bad thing, and must moreover be really tiring for those who were indulging in it.* The comedy of the situation lit up every mind like a lightning flash. The merriment increased. 'This *overacting* may be good for you,' he said, 'but not for me.' – 'So long as it's good for us,' replied one of the sick men selfishly. Not knowing whether he was among real madmen or people pretending to be mad, our hero thought it would be most sensible to leave, but someone locked the door and hid the key. Another, falling to his knees before him, begged his pardon in the name of the society, and declared to him insolently, but with tears in his eyes, that despite his spiritual inferiority, which did perhaps arouse a certain pity, all were filled with the feelings of the deepest friendship towards him. He resigned himself to staying, and even condescended, at their insistent requests, to play a little music. But as the sounds of the violin spread through the apartment like a new contagion, they took hold (the word is hardly too strong) of first one sick man, then another. The room was filled with deep, raucous sighs, sudden sobs, silent floods of tears. The horrified musician stopped, and going up to the man whose bliss was expressing itself most noisily, he asked him if he was in great pain and what would help to relieve it. One of those present, a practical man, suggested lemonade and acids. But the sick man, his eyes gleaming ecstatically, looked at them both with unspeakable contempt. Fancy wanting to save a man sick with too much life, sick with joy!

As can be seen from this anecdote, benevolence occupies quite a large place in the sensations caused by hashish; a languid, lazy, mute benevolence derived from the slackening of the nerves. In support of this observation, someone once told me of an adventure that had befallen him in this state of intoxication, and as he had retained a very precise memory of his sensations, I understood perfectly well into what grotesque and inexplicable quandary this difference in range and level of intelligence I mentioned just now had thrown him. I do not remember if it was on the first or second experience of the man in question. Had he taken too strong a dose, or had hashish produced, without the help of any other apparent cause (something that often happens), much more vigorous effects? He told me that in the midst of his pleasure, that supreme pleasure of feeling full of life and believing oneself to be filled with genius, he had all of a sudden encountered a terrifying object. At first dazzled by the beauty of his sensations, he had suddenly been deeply alarmed by them. He had wondered what would happen to his intelligence and his physical organs, if this state, which he took to be a supernatural state, were to become yet more exacerbated, if his nerves were to become ever more delicate. Thanks to the power of magnification possessed by the sick man's spiritual eye, this fear must be an inexpressible torment.

'I was,' he said, 'like a horse swept away and running towards an abyss, wanting to stop, but quite unable to do so. It was a perfectly fearful gallop and my thought, in thrall to circumstances, to the environment, to accidental factors and to everything implied by the word 'chance', had taken a purely and absolutely rhapsodic turn. "It's too late!" I kept repeating to myself in despair. When this feeling ended, after what seemed to me an infinite time although it occupied perhaps only a few minutes, when I was finally able to plunge into the bliss, so dear to Orientals, which follows this phase of rage and fury, I was overwhelmed by a new distress. A new disquiet, perfectly trivial and puerile, overcame me. I suddenly remembered that I had been invited to dinner at a gathering of serious-minded men. I could already imagine myself in the midst of a well-mannered, discreet crowd, in which everyone would be in perfect control of himself, being obliged to take great care to conceal my state of mind under the gleam of the numerous lamps. I was convinced that I would succeed, but I also felt myself almost fainting away at the thought of the efforts of will-power I would have to deploy. By I don't know what accident, the words of the Gospel – "Woe to that man by whom the offence cometh!" – had just sprung to my memory, and while trying to forget them, by virtue of the very efforts I was making to forget them, I kept on repeating them in my mind. My distress (for it was a real distress) then took on grandiose proportions. I resolved, in spite of my weakness, to take a drastic step and consult a pharmacist; for I didn't know anything about reagents and I wanted to go out with a clear and detached mind into society, where my duty called me. But on the threshold of the pharmacist's, a sudden thought struck me, bringing me to a halt for a few minutes and forcing me to reflect. I had just looked at myself, in passing, in the glass of a shop window, and my face had really surprised me. That pallor, those pinched lips, those bulging eyes! "I'm going to bother that worthy man," I said to myself, "and for what a silly reason!" Add to this the sense of seeming ridiculous that I wished to avoid, and the fear of finding people in the shop. But my sudden benevolence for this unknown apothecary dominated all my other feelings. I imagined this man to be as sensitive as I myself was at this fateful moment, and, as I also imagined that his ear and his soul must, like mine, vibrate at the slightest sound, I resolved to enter his shop on tiptoe. "I can't," I said to myself, "show too much discretion towards a man whose charity I am about to impose on." And then I promised to extinguish the sound of my voice as I had my footsteps; do you know it, this voice of hashish? Grave, deep, guttural, and greatly resembling that of old opium eaters. The result was the opposite of the one I wished to obtain. Intent on reassuring the pharmacist, I merely frightened him. He knew nothing about this illness, had never heard of it. And yet he was gazing at me with a curiosity in which was a heavy admixture of mistrust. Did he take me for a madman, a malefactor or a beggar? For none of these things, no doubt;

but all these absurd ideas darted through my brain. I was obliged to explain to him at great length (and with what exhausting effort!) the nature of hemp jelly and the use to which it is put, repeating to him again and again that there was no danger, that there was, *for him*, no reason to get alarmed, and that I was merely asking for some means of assuaging or counteracting the effects, insisting several times over how sincerely sorry I was to be causing him any bother. Finally – you must try to understand all the humiliation contained for me in these words – he begged me simply *to take myself off*. Such was the recompense for my exaggerated charity and benevolence. I went along to my gathering; I gave offence to nobody. No one guessed at the superhuman efforts I was forced to make to resemble everyone else. But I will never forget the tortures inflicted by an ultra-poetic intoxication, one that was constrained by decorum and thwarted by a sense of duty!'

Although by nature inclined to sympathise with all the pains born of imagination, I could not prevent myself from laughing at this story. The man who told it to me has not changed his ways. He has continued to want the cursed jelly to provide him with the stimulus one should find in oneself; but as he is a prudent man, well-mannered, a man of the world, he has diminished the doses, which has enabled him to increase their frequency. He will come to realise, later on, the rotten fruit of his regimen.

I must return to the way the intoxication usually develops. After this first phase of childlike gaiety, there is as it were a momentary calm. But new developments soon manifest themselves through a chill sensation in the extremities (which may even become a very intense cold in certain individuals) and a great weakness in every limb; then you have butter-fingers, and in your head, in your whole being, you feel a cumbersome stupor and stupefaction. Your eyes bulge more and more; they are as it were pulled in every direction by an implacable ecstasy. Pallor floods over your face. Your lips become pinched and are pulled back into your mouth, with that shortness of breath characteristic of the ambitiousness of a man in the grip of great projects, oppressed by vast thoughts, or taking a deep breath before launching himself into his run. Your throat contracts, so to speak. Your palate is parched by a thirst it would be infinitely sweet to satisfy, if the delights of sloth were not more pleasant and did not act as a drag on the least bodily exertion. Deep, raucous sighs emerge from your breast, as if your *former* body could not sustain the desires and the activity of your *new* soul. From time to time, a shudder passes through you and makes you twitch involuntarily, like those sudden starts which, at the end of a day's work or during a stormy night, precede definitive sleep.

Before going any further, I wish, in regard to that sensation of chill I mentioned earlier, to narrate another anecdote which will serve to show the extent to which the effects, even the purely physical effects, can vary from individual to individual. This time it is a man of letters speaking, and in a few passages in his account you will, I think, be able to detect the signs of a literary temperament.

'I had,' he told me, 'taken a moderate dose of fatty extract, and everything was going perfectly well. The fit of unhealthy gaiety had lasted only briefly, and I found myself in a state of listlessness and astonishment which was almost happiness. So I was able to promise myself a tranquil and carefree evening. Unfortunately it so happened that I was forced to accompany someone to the theatre. I made up my mind to put a brave face on it, being resolved to disguise my immense desire for sloth and immobility. All the carriages in my part of town were already taken, so I had to resign myself to making a long journey on foot, picking my way through the discordant din of the carriages, the stupid conversations of the passers-by, a whole ocean of trivialities. A slight chill had already started to affect my fingertips; soon it changed into a very intense cold, as if my two hands were plunged into a bucket of icy water. But it caused no suffering; this almost acute sensation penetrated me, rather, in a very pleasurable way. And yet it seemed to me that this cold was permeating me more and more, as I continued on that interminable journey. Two or three times I asked the person I was accompanying if it really was cold; the reply came that on the contrary, the temperature was more than mild. Once I was finally settled in the theatre, enclosed in the box reserved for me, with two or three hours of rest stretching out ahead of me, I thought I had reached the promised land. The feelings I had repressed on the way there, with all the paltry energy I could muster, then erupted, and I abandoned myself freely to my mute frenzy. The cold was still increasing, and yet I could see people in only light clothing, or even wiping their brows with an air of tiredness. The amusing idea struck me that I was a privileged man to whom alone the right had been granted to be cold in a theatre in the middle of summer. This cold was growing to the point of becoming alarming; but I was before all else dominated by the desire to know how low it could sink. Finally it reached such a point, became so complete and so general, that all my thoughts froze, so to speak; I was a thinking piece of ice; I felt myself to be a statue carved from a single icy block; and this crazy hallucination gave me such pride, and aroused in me such a sense of mental well-being, that I would find it impossible to define for you. What added to my abominable pleasure was

the certainty that all those present were unaware of my nature
and the superiority I had over them; and on top of that was the
happiness of thinking that my friend hadn't for a single minute
suspected the bizarre sensations that possessed me! I was
enjoying the reward for my dissimulation, and my exceptional
pleasure was a real secret.

'Furthermore, hardly had I entered my box than my eyes
had been struck by an impression of darkness which seemed
to me to have some relation to the idea of cold. It may well be
that these two ideas lent strength to each other. You know that
hashish always evokes magnificent constructions of light,
glorious and splendid visions, cascades of liquid gold; all light
is good for it, the light that streams down like a shimmering
waterfall and the light which catches like spangles on points
and rough surfaces, the candelabra of salons, the candles of
the month of Mary, the avalanches of pink in sunsets. It seems
that the wretched chandelier there shed a light quite
insufficient for my insatiable thirst for light; I thought I was
entering, as I told you, into a world of darkness, that moreover
grew gradually thicker, while I dreamt of polar nights and
eternal winters. As for the stage (it was a theatre devoted to
comedy), it alone was luminous, infinitely small and situated
far, far away, as at the end of an immense stereoscope. I won't
claim that I was listening to the actors, you know that's
impossible; from time to time my thought picked up in
passing a fragmentary phrase, and, like a skilled dancer, used it
as a trampoline to bounce off into the most exotic daydreams.
You might suppose that a drama, heard in this fashion, would
lack logic and coherence; don't you believe it; I was able to
discover a very subtle meaning in the drama created by my
absent-minded reverie. Nothing in it shocked me, and I was
rather similar to that poet who, watching a performance of

Esther for the first time, found it perfectly natural that Haman should declare his love to the queen. It was, as you will have guessed, the moment when the latter in fact throws himself at Esther's feet to implore her to forgive his crimes. If all dramas were interpreted in accordance with this method, they would gain greatly in beauty, even those of Racine.

'The actors seemed to me excessively tiny and surrounded by a precise, meticulous outline, like the figures in Meissonier's paintings. I could distinctly make out, not only the most minute details of their attire, such as the design of the fabric, stitches, buttons, etc., but even the line of separation between their false foreheads and their real ones, the white, blue, and red patches and the rest of their make-up. And those Lilliputians were arrayed in a cold, magical clarity, like that which a very clean pane of glass imparts to an oil-painting. When I was finally able to emerge from this vault of icy darkness, and as soon as the interior phantasmagoria had dispersed and I had come back to my senses, I felt a greater weariness than any stressful, demanding piece of work has ever caused me.'

It is indeed in this period of intoxication that a new delicacy, a greater acuteness in all the senses, appears. Smell, sight, hearing, touch are all equally affected by this improvement. Your eyes can scan the infinite. Your ears can perceive almost imperceptible sounds amid the loudest din. It is at this point that the hallucinations begin. External objects slowly and successively assume strange appearances; they become deformed and transformed. Then come the equivocations, the mistakes, and the transpositions of ideas. Sounds are decked out in colours, and colours contain their own music. This is perfectly natural, you will say, and any poetic brain, in its healthy normal state, can conceive these analogies. But I have already warned the reader that there is nothing positively supernatural in the intoxication wrought by hashish; it is just that these analogies then take on an unaccustomed vividness; they penetrate, they invade, they overwhelm the mind with their despotic character. Musical notes become numbers, and if your mind is gifted with any aptitude for mathematics, any melody or harmony you listen to, while it retains its voluptuous, sensual character, is transformed into a vast arithmetical operation, in which numbers engender more numbers, and you can follow their phases and their generation with an inexplicable ease and an agility equal to that of the performer.

It sometimes happens that your personality disappears, and objectivity, that characteristic of pantheistic poets, becomes so abnormally developed in you that the contemplation of external objects makes you forget your own existence, and you soon merge into them. Your eye falls on a tree bending harmoniously in the breeze; in a few seconds, what in the brain of a poet would merely be a completely natural comparison becomes in yours a reality. At first you project onto the tree your passions, your desire or your melancholy; its groanings and swayings become yours, and soon you *are* the tree. Likewise, the bird hovering in the depths of the blue sky represents at first the immortal longing to hover over human affairs; but already you are the bird itself. Let's suppose you are sitting down smoking. Your attention will come to rest a little too long on the bluish clouds rising from the pipe. The idea of a certain evaporation, slow, successive, eternal, takes hold of your mind, and you are soon applying this idea to your own thoughts, to your own thinking matter. By a strange equivocation, by a kind of transposition or intellectual misunderstanding, you feel yourself evaporating too, and you attribute to your pipe (in which you feel that you are squatting, all tamped down like the tobacco) the strange activity of *smoking you.*

Fortunately, this interminable imagining has lasted only a minute, for an interval of lucidity has enabled you, with a great effort, to examine the clock. But another stream of ideas sweeps you away; it will sweep you away for another minute in its living whirlpool, and this other minute will be yet another eternity. For the proportions of time and being are completely distorted by the multitude and intensity of sensations and ideas. You seem to live several human lives in the space of an hour. Are you not then similar to a fantastic novel, one that is alive rather than written? There is no longer any proportion between your physical organs and the intense pleasures they experience; and it is above all from this consideration that arises one's disapproval of this dangerous exercise in which freedom disappears.

When I say 'hallucinations', the word is not to be taken in its strictest sense. There is a very significant if subtle distinction between the pure hallucination of the kind doctors often have occasion to study, and the hallucination, or rather the confusion between different sense-impressions, in the mental state caused by hashish. In the first case, hallucination is sudden, perfect and inevitable; furthermore, it finds no pretext or excuse in the world of external objects. The patient sees a shape, or hears sounds, where they do not in fact exist. In the second case, hallucination is progressive, almost voluntary, and becomes perfect and fully ripened only by the action of the imagination. Finally, it has a pretext. Sound will speak, will say distinct things, but there was a sound to start with. The intoxicated eyes of the man in a hashish trance will see strange shapes; but, before being strange or monstrous, these shapes were simple and natural. The intensity, the quite eloquent vividness of the hallucination produced by intoxication in no way invalidates this fundamental difference. The hashish hallucination has its roots in the current environment and the present time, the other sort does not.

So as to give a clearer sense of this ebullience of the imagination, this blossoming of the dream and this poetic procreation to which is condemned a brain intoxicated by hashish, I will recount another anecdote. This time, it's not an idle young man speaking, nor is it a man of letters; it's a woman, a woman of maturer years, curious, excitable of spirit who, having yielded to the desire to become acquainted with the poison, is describing to another lady the most significant of her visions in the following terms. I will transcribe her account literally:

'However strange and novel the sensations I derived from my twelve-hour madness (twelve or twenty? to tell you the truth, I have no idea), I will not dwell on them any further. The spiritual arousal is too acute, the resulting fatigue too great; and, in short, I think there is something criminal in this puerility. Finally I yielded to curiosity; and then it was an act of shared madness, at the home of some old friends, where I didn't see anything very wrong in losing face a little. Before anything else, I have to tell you that this cursed hashish is a particularly perfidious substance; you sometimes feel that you have put the intoxication behind you, but it's merely an illusory calm. There are short respites, and then it takes over again. So, towards ten o'clock in the evening, I found myself in one of those momentary states; I thought I had been delivered from that superabundance of life that had given me so many pleasures, it's true, but which was not without its sense of disquiet and fear. I was glad to sit down to supper, as if exhausted after a long journey. For up until then, out of caution, I had abstained from eating. But, even before leaving the table, my delirium had caught up with me, like a cat catching up with a mouse, and the poison started once more to play tricks with my poor brain. Although my house is only a short distance from the château of my friends, and there was a carriage laid on for me, I felt so overwhelmed by the need to dream and to abandon myself to that irresistible madness that I accepted with joy their offer to put me up there until morning. You know the château; you know that all the part inhabited by the masters of the place has been arranged, decorated and cheered up in modern style, but that the part generally uninhabited has been left as it was, with its old style and its old decor. It was decided that they would improvise a bedroom for me in this part of the château, and to this end they chose the smallest bedroom, a kind of boudoir, somewhat decrepit and faded but nonetheless charming. I must describe it to you as well as I can, so that you'll be able to understand the strange vision of which I was the victim, a vision which occupied me for an entire night, without me having the leisure to notice the hours gliding by.

'This boudoir is very small, very narrow. Up on the level of the cornice the ceiling is rounded into a vault; the walls are covered with long, narrow mirrors, separated by panels on which are painted landscapes like the slovenly backdrops in stage scenery. On the cornice on all four walls are depicted various allegorical figures, some of them in attitudes of repose, others running or fluttering around. Above them, a few brilliant birds and some flowers. Behind the figures rises a trellis painted in *trompe-l'oeil*, naturally following the curve of the ceiling. This ceiling is gilded. All the interstices between the beading and the figures are thus covered in gold, and in the middle the gold is interrupted only by the geometric network of the imaginary trellis. You can see that it bears some resemblance to a very distinguished cage, a very fine cage for a very big bird. I should add that the night was very fine, crystal-clear, and the moon very bright, so much so that, even when I had extinguished the candle, all this decoration remained visible, not illumined by the eye of my spirit as you might think, but lit up by this beautiful night whose glimmerings were caught on all the embroidery of gold, mirrors and kaleidoscopic colours.

'I was at first completely astonished to see great spaces stretching out in front of me, next to me, on every side; there were limpid rivers and verdant landscapes gazing at their reflections in tranquil waters. You can guess at the effect created here by the panels repeated in the mirrors. On looking up, I saw a setting sun that resembled molten metal as it cools. This was the gold of the ceiling; but the trellis made me think that I was in a kind of cage or house open to the free space on every side, and that only the bars of my magnificent prison separated me from all these wonders. At first I started laughing at my illusion; but the more I gazed at it, the more the magic intensified, and the more full of life, crystal-clear and despotically real it became. From that point on, the idea of confinement dominated my mind, without adversely affecting overmuch, I have to say, the varied pleasures that I was drawing from the spectacle draped all around and above me. I imagined that I was to be shut away for a long time, for thousands of years perhaps, in that sumptuous cage, amidst those enchanting landscapes, between those wonderful horizons. I dreamt of the *Sleeping Beauty*, of an atonement to perform, of future deliverance. Above my head fluttered brilliant tropical birds, and, as my ear perceived the sound of the little bells on the necks of the horses wending their way along the main road in the distance, the two senses melding their impressions into a single idea, I attributed to the birds that mysterious coppery song, and I thought that they were singing from metal throats. Of course they were conversing about me and celebrating my captivity. Gambolling monkeys, and clownish satyrs seemed to be amused by the plight of that prisoner lying there condemned to immobility. But all the mythological divinities were gazing at me with charming smiles, as if to encourage me to bear the spell patiently, and it was as if their irises swivelled to the corner of their eyes to catch my glance. I concluded from this that if former misdeeds, a few sins unknown even to myself, had necessarily brought about this temporary punishment, I could nonetheless count on a higher goodness, which, while condemning me to prudence, would offer me more substantial pleasures than the pleasures we derive from our dolls throughout our girlhood. You can see that moral considerations were not absent from my dream; but I have to confess that the pleasure of contemplating these shapes and brilliant colours, and of believing myself to be the centre of a fantastic drama, frequently absorbed all my other thoughts. This state lasted a long time, a very long time… Did it last until morning? I don't know. I suddenly saw the morning sun ensconced in my bedroom; I felt a profound astonishment, and in spite of all my efforts to remember, it was impossible for me to know whether I had slept or whether I had patiently been suffering a delightful insomnia. Just now it had been night, and now it was day! And yet I had lived a long time, such a long time!… The notion of time or rather the ability to measure time had been abolished, and so I had been able to measure the entire night only by the multitude of my thoughts. However long it appeared to me from this point of view, it still seemed that it had lasted just a few seconds, or even that it hadn't taken place in eternity.

'I haven't mentioned my fatigue... it was immense. They say that the enthusiasm of poets and creators resembles what I felt, although I have always imagined that the people whose task it is to inspire emotions in us must be endowed with a perfectly calm temperament; but if poetic delirium resembles that which a small spoonful of jelly procured in me, I think that the pleasures of the public cost the poets dear, and it was not without a certain well-being, a prosaic satisfaction, that I finally felt myself to be back at home, in my intellectual home, I mean real life.'

So speaks a woman of obvious good sense; but we will use her story merely to derive from it a few useful notes that will complete this quite summary description of the principal sensations produced by hashish.

She spoke of supper as a pleasure arriving just at the right time, when a momentary, though apparently definitive, lull enabled her to return to real life. There are indeed, as I have said, intermittent periods and deceptive calms, and hashish often provokes a voracious hunger, and almost always an excessive thirst. But dinner or supper, instead of inaugurating a definitive period of repose, produce that new and intensified outbreak, that attack of vertigo which the lady complained about, one followed by a series of enchanting visions, tinged with a slight feeling of fright, to which she resigned herself in a positive frame of mind and with real good grace.

The afore-mentioned tyrannical hunger and thirst cannot be satisfied without a certain labour. For man feels so elevated above material things, or rather so prostrated by his intoxication, that he needs to put a great deal of time and effort into moving a bottle or a fork.

The definitive crisis caused by the digestion of food is indeed very violent: it is impossible to struggle against it; and such a state would be intolerable if it lasted too long and did not soon give way to another phase of the intoxication, which, in the above case, manifested itself by splendid visions, mildly terrifying and at the same time full of consolations. This new state is what Orientals call 'kief'. It is no longer something swirling and tumultuous; it is a calm and immobile bliss, a glorious resignation. For a long time now you have ceased to be in control of yourself, but you are no longer afflicted by this. Pain and the idea of time have disappeared, or if they sometimes dare to make their presence felt, it is only insofar as they are transfigured by the dominant sensation, and then they are, in relation to their usual shape, what poetic melancholy is in relation to positive pain.

But, before all else, let us note that in this lady's story (it was with this aim in mind that I transcribed it), the hallucination is of a mixed kind, and takes its impetus from the spectacle of external things; the mind is merely a mirror in which the environment is reflected, transformed in an outrageous fashion. Then, we see the occurrence of what I would be tempted to call moral hallucination: the subject believes he or she is being forced to undergo an atonement; but the feminine temperament, which is not really given to analysis, did not allow her to note the strangely optimistic character of the said hallucination. The benevolent gaze of the divinities of Olympia is poeticised by a veneer which is essentially *hashishin*. I won't go so far as to say that this lady felt more than a twinge of remorse, but her thoughts, having momentarily turned towards melancholy and regret, were rapidly coloured by hope. This is a remark we will have further opportunity to verify.

She mentioned the fatigue she felt the following day; this fatigue is indeed profound, but it doesn't manifest itself immediately and, when you are forced to acknowledge it, it is not without some astonishment. For at first, when you have fully realised that a new day has risen on the horizon of your life, you feel an astonishing sense of well-being; you seem to enjoy a marvellous lightness of spirit. But no sooner have you got up than an old trace of your intoxicated state pursues you and holds you back. Your tottering legs carry you cautiously, you are frightened at every moment that you might break like some fragile object. A profound languor (there are people who claim it is not without its charm) overwhelms your mind and spreads through your faculties like a mist through the landscape. There you are, for another few hours, incapable of work, action or energy. This is the punishment for the impious prodigality with which you have spent your nervous fluid. You have cast your personality to the four winds of heaven, and now, how hard it is for you to put it together again and focus it!

4
THE GOD-MAN

It's time to leave aside all those conjuring tricks and those great puppets born from the fumes of childish brains. Shouldn't we be talking about graver things: the modifications of human feelings, and, in a word, of the *ethics* of hashish?

Up until now, I have written merely an abridged monograph on intoxication; I have restricted myself to emphasising its main characteristics, especially its material characteristics. But what is more important, I believe, for the spiritual man, is to be aware of the action of the poison on man's spiritual part – in other words the magnification, deformation and exaggeration of his habitual feelings and his moral perceptions, which then present, in an exceptional atmosphere, a real phenomenon of refraction.

The man who, having indulged in hashish or opium for a long time, has managed, enfeebled as he has become by the habit of his bondage, to find the necessary energy to free himself, is in my view an escaped prisoner. He inspires me with more admiration than the cautious man who has never succumbed, having always taken care to avoid temptation. The English often use, in connection with opium eaters, terms which can appear excessive only to those innocents unacquainted with the horrors of that degenerate state: *enchained, fettered, enslaved!* Chains, indeed, next to which all others – the chains of duty, the chains of illegitimate love – are merely tissues of gauze, or spider's webs! 'I had become a bounden slave in the trammels of opium, and my labours and my orders had taken a colouring from my dreams,' says the husband of Ligeia; but in how many wonderful passages does Edgar Allan Poe, that incomparable poet, that irrefutable philosopher, to whom reference must always be made when the mysterious maladies of the soul are mentioned, describe the dark and captivating splendours of opium? The lover of the bright Berenice, Egaeus the metaphysician, speaks of a weakening of his faculties, which forces him to attach an abnormal, monstrous significance to the simplest phenomena: 'To muse for long unwearied hours with my attention riveted to some frivolous device on the margin, or in the typography of a book; to become absorbed for the better part of a summer's day in a quaint shadow falling aslant upon the tapestry, or upon the floor; to lose myself for an entire night in watching the steady flame of a lamp, or the embers of a fire; to dream away whole days over the perfume of a flower; to repeat monotonously some common word, until the sound, by dint of frequent repetition, ceased to convey any idea whatever to the mind; to lose all sense of motion or physical existence, by means of absolute bodily quiescence long and obstinately persevered in: such were a few of the most common and least pernicious vagaries induced by a condition of the mental faculties, not, indeed, altogether unparalleled, but certainly bidding defiance to anything like analysis or explanation'. And the nerve-sick Augustus Bedloe who, every day before his morning walk, swallows his dose of opium, admits to us that the main benefit he derives from this daily poisoning is that he takes an exaggerated interest in everything, even of the most trivial kind: 'In the meantime the morphine had its customary effect – that of enduing all the external world with an intensity of interest. In the quivering of a leaf – in the hue of a blade of grass – in the shape of a trefoil – in the humming of a bee – in the gleaming of a dewdrop – in the breathing of the wind – in the faint odours that came from the forest – there came a whole universe of suggestion – a gay and motley train of rhapsodies and immethodical thought'.[5]

In these words does the master of horror, the prince of mystery, express himself through the mouth of one of his characters. These two characteristics of opium are perfectly applicable to hashish; in both cases, the intelligence, formerly free, now becomes enslaved; but the word 'rhapsodic', which so well defines a train of ideas suggested and dictated by the external world and the fortuitous arrangement of circumstances, has a truer and more terrible accuracy in the case of hashish. Here, one's reasoning is merely a wreck at the mercy of every current, and the train of ideas is *infinitely more* accelerated and more *rhapsodic*. This is, I believe, a sufficiently clear indication of how hashish is, in its effects, much more vehement than opium, much more inimical to a regular life, in short, much more disturbing. I do not know whether ten years of hashish intoxication will bring in their wake disasters equal to those caused by ten years of opium eating; I will just say that, as far as its immediate effects on the present and the following day are concerned, hashish has much deadlier effects; the one is an easy-going seducer, the other a dissolute demon.

I wish, in this final part, to define and analyse the moral ravage caused by this dangerous and delightful gymnastics, a ravage so great, and a danger so profound, that those who return from the combat only lightly wounded seem to me like brave men who have escaped from the cave of a multiform Proteus, each one an Orpheus who has vanquished Hell. You may, if you will, take this form of language as an excessive metaphor, but I must confess that poisonous stimulants seem to me not only one of the most terrible and most dangerous means at the disposal of the Spirit of Darkness in his attempt to enlist and enslave pitiable mankind, but even one of his most perfect incarnations.

This time, to shorten my task and make my analysis clearer, instead of bringing together scattered anecdotes, I will amass a large number of observations to do with one single fictitious character. I thus need to imagine a soul of my own choosing. In his *Confessions*, De Quincey correctly asserts that opium, instead of sending people to sleep, acts as a stimulant, but stimulates them only in accordance with their nature, so that, to pass judgement on the wonders of opium, it would be absurd to refer to a cattle-dealer's experiences of it; for such a man will simply dream of cattle and pasture. Now I don't intend to describe the cumbrous fantasies of a cattle-breeder intoxicated with hashish; who would read them with pleasure? Who would even be prepared to read them? To idealise my subject, I must focus all its rays within a single circle, I must polarise them; and the tragic circle in which I am going to bring them together will, as I have said, be a soul of my choosing, something analogous to what the eighteenth century called the 'man of sensibility', what the romantic school called the 'misunderstood man', and what families and the mass of the bourgeoisie generally brand with the epithet 'original'.

A half-nervous, half-bilious temperament, that is the one most favourable to the development of an intoxication of this kind; we may add a cultivated mind, well-practised in the study of shape and colour; a tender heart, worn out by misfortune, but still ready and willing to be rejuvenated; we will, if you have no objection, go so far as to admit some former misdeeds, and, as must result from an easily excitable nature, if not real remorse, at least a regret for the time that has been profaned and put to no good use. A taste for metaphysics, an awareness of the different hypotheses of philosophy concerning human destiny, are certainly complements not to be sneezed at – nor is that love of virtue, of abstract, stoic or mystical virtue, which is posited in all the books from which modern childhood draws its nourishment as the highest peak to which a distinguished soul can ascend. If you add to all this a great subtlety of the senses which I omitted as a supererogatory condition, I believe I have brought together the most common general elements of the modern man of sensibility, of what might be called the 'common form of originality'. Let us now see what will become of this individuality when pushed to extremes by hashish. Let us follow that procession of the human imagination as far as its last and most splendid altar of repose, the belief of the individual in his or her own divinity.

If you are one of these souls, your innate love of shape and colour will at first find an immense pasture in the first developments of your intoxication. Colours will take on an unaccustomed vigour and will enter your brain with an all-conquering intensity. Whether delicate, mediocre, or even just plain bad, the paintings on the ceiling will be endowed with a startling vivacity; the coarsest wallpaper on the walls of inns will gain in depth, producing splendid dioramas. Nymphs with dazzling flesh gaze at you with wide eyes, deeper and more limpid than the sky and the water; characters from antiquity, attired in their priestly or military costumes, exchange solemn confidences with you at a mere glance. The sinuous curving of outline is a language now finally made clear in which you can read the agitation and the desires of people's souls. Meanwhile you develop a mysterious and temporary state of mind, in which the profundity of life, bristling with its multiple problems, is entirely revealed in the spectacle, however natural and trivial it may be, that lies before your eyes – in which the first object to present itself becomes an eloquent symbol. Fourier and Swedenborg, the one with his *analogies*, the other with his *correspondences*, have become embodied in the vegetable or animal forms that your gaze alights on, and instead of divulging their teachings in words, they indoctrinate you by shape and colour. Allegorical understanding assumes within you proportions hitherto unknown; we may note, in passing, that allegory, that so *spiritual* genre, which inept painters have accustomed us to despise, but which is really one of the primitive and most natural forms of poetry, resumes its legitimate dominion in an intelligence enlightened by intoxication. Then hashish spreads across the whole of life like a magical veneer; it paints it in solemn colours and illuminates it in all its depth. Landscapes with jagged outlines, receding horizons, prospects of cities made white by the cadaverous livid glow of a storm, or lit up by the concentrated gleam of setting suns – a spatial depth, and an allegory of temporal depth – the dances, gestures and declamations of the actors, if you have taken refuge in a theatre – the first sentence that springs to your eyes, if you glance at a book – everything, in fact, the totality of beings in the universe rises before you with a new and hitherto unsuspected glory. Grammar, arid grammar itself, becomes something like an evocative sorcery; words rise from the grave clothed in flesh and bones, the substantive, in its substantial majesty, the adjective, a transparent garment which clothes and colours it like a glaze, and the verb, the angel of movement, which sets the sentence in motion. Music, another language dear to the indolent or profound minds which seek relaxation by varying their work, speaks to you of yourself and narrates the poem of your life; it becomes of one body with you, and you melt into it. It expresses your passion, not in a vague and indefinite way, as it does on those evenings you spend lolling at the opera, but in a detailed, positive way, every movement in the rhythm indicating a movement familiar to your soul, every note transforming itself into a word, and the whole poem entering your brain like a dictionary endowed with life.

You mustn't believe that all these phenomena are produced in the mind pell-mell, with the shrill accents of reality and the disarray of external life. The inner eye transforms everything and gives everything the complement of beauty that it lacks if it is really to seem attractive. It is also to this essentially voluptuous and sensual phase that belongs the love of limpid water, flowing or stagnant, that is so astonishingly pronounced in the mental intoxication of a few artists. Mirrors become a pretext for that reverie which resembles a spiritual thirst, joined to the physical thirst which parches the throat, and which I mentioned earlier; waters rippling by, fountains playing, harmonious waterfalls, the blue immensity of the sea, roll, sing, sleep with an inexpressible charm. The water spreads out like a real enchantress, and, although I do not set great store by the tales of people going berserk under the influence of hashish, I wouldn't deny that the contemplation of a limpid abyss is somewhat dangerous for a mind in love with space and crystal clarity, and that the old fable of Undine might well become, for the devotee, a tragic reality.

I think I have dwelt sufficiently on the monstrous extension of time and space, two ideas that are always linked, but which the mind in this state can confront without sadness and without fear. It gazes with a certain melancholy delight through the depth of the years, and boldly sinks into the infinite prospects that open up. You will have guessed, I presume, that this abnormal and tyrannical extension applies equally to all feelings and all ideas: thus it applies to benevolence; I have, I think, given quite a fine example of this; the same is true of love. The idea of beauty must naturally come to occupy a huge place in a spiritual temperament of the kind I have supposed. Harmony, the swaying of the lines, eurhythmic movements, appear to the dreamer as necessities, as duties, not merely for every being in creation, but for himself, the dreamer who finds himself, at this moment of the crisis, endowed with a wonderful aptitude for understanding this immortal and universal rhythm. And if our fanatic is lacking in personal beauty, don't think that he will suffer for long from his forced recognition of this fact, nor that he will view himself as a discordant note in the world of harmony and beauty improvised by his imagination. The sophisms of hashish are numerous and admirable, tending generally to optimism, and one of the principle ones, the most effective, is that which transforms desire into reality. The same is doubtless true in many cases of ordinary life, but here it happens with so much more ardour and subtlety! Furthermore, how could a being so highly gifted in the understanding of harmony, a sort of priest of the Beautiful, constitute an exception and a blemish in his own theory? Moral beauty and its power, grace and its seductions, eloquence and its exploits, all these ideas soon present themselves as able to correct an indiscreet ugliness and then to bring consolation, and finally to act as the perfect flatterers of an imaginary sceptre.

As for love, I have heard many people, impelled by the same curiosity as a schoolboy, trying to discover the facts from those already familiar with hashish. What happens to that intoxication of love, already so powerful in its natural state, when it is enclosed in the other intoxication, like a sun within another sun? This is the question that will spring to the minds of a host of people I will call the gapers and gawpers of the intellectual world. In response to an indecent insinuation, implicit in that part of the question which people do not dare formulate explicitly, I will refer the reader to Pliny, who has spoken somewhere of the properties of hemp in a way bound to make many illusions evaporate. It is well-known, furthermore, that lifeless apathy is the most ordinary result of the way men abuse their nerves and the substances that stimulate them. Now, as there is here no question of any effective potency, but of emotion or susceptibility, I will simply beg the reader to consider that the imagination of a highly strung man, intoxicated by hashish, is intensified to a fantastic level, as difficult to determine as the maximum possible strength of the wind in a hurricane, and his senses made subtle to a degree almost equally difficult to determine. It is thus permissible to believe that a gentle caress, the most innocent of all, a hand-shake for instance, can have a value multiplied a hundredfold by one's current state of soul and senses, and lead them per-haps, very rapidly in fact, to that brief fainting fit considered by vulgar mortals as the *summum bonum* of happiness. But the fact that, in an imagination often occupied by matters of love, hashish awakens tender memories, to which pain and unhappiness even add new lustre, cannot be doubted. It is no less certain that a strong dose of sensuality is mingled with these agitations of the mind; and furthermore, it is not irre-levant to note something that would be enough to demonstrate on this point the immorality of hashish: a sect of Ismailis (it is from the Ismailis that are sprung the Assassins) perverted its worship far beyond that of the impartial linga, to the absolute and exclusive worship of the feminine half of the symbol. It would be perfectly natural, as each man is a representation of history, to see an obscene heresy, a monstrous religion produced in a mind that has cravenly delivered itself into the mercy of an infernal drug, and which smiles at the dissipation of its own faculties.

Since we have observed that the intoxication of hashish creates a strange benevolence even towards people we do not know, a kind of philanthropy that consists of pity rather than love (it is here that the first germ of the satanic spirit shows itself, soon developing in an extraordinary manner), but goes so far as to make us afraid of hurting anyone at all, it is easy to guess at what becomes of a more specific romantic attach-ment, one whose object is a cherished person who has played or plays an important role in the mental life of the patient.

Worship, adoration, prayer, dreams of happiness are spun and flung out with the ambitious energy and explosive brilliance of a firework display; like the powder and the multicoloured flashes of the display, they produce a dazzling light and vanish into the darkness. There is no combination and permutation of feelings to which the supple love of a slave of hashish cannot lend itself. A desire to protect the other, a feeling of ardent and devoted paternity can be mixed with a culpable sensuality which hashish will always be able to excuse and absolve. It goes even further. Imagine wrongdoings previously committed that have left bitter traces in the soul, a husband or a lover contemplating with mere sadness (in his normal state) a past overshadowed by storm clouds; the bitterness can in this state change into sweetness; the need for forgiveness makes the imagination more inventive and more suppliant, and remorse itself, in this diabolical drama that finds expression in the sole form of a long monologue, can act as a stimulant and powerfully fan the flames of the heart's enthusiasm. Yes, remorse! Was I wrong to say that hashish appeared, to a really philosophical mind, as a perfectly satanic instrument? Remorse, a strange ingredient of pleasure, is soon drowned out in the delightful contemplation of remorse, in a kind of voluptuous analysis; and this analysis is so rapid that man, that natural devil – to speak like the Swedenborgians – does not realise how involuntary it is and how much, from second to second, it grows closer to diabolical perfection. He admires his remorse and glories in himself, while in the very process of losing his freedom.

So here we have the man I imagined, the spirit of my choosing, having reached that degree of joy and serenity in which he is constrained to admire himself. All contradiction is erased, all philosophical problems become limpid, or at least appear so. Everything is the raw material for intense pleasure. The plenitude of his current life inspires him with immoderate pride. A voice speaks within him (alas! it is his own) which tells him: 'You now have the right to consider yourself as superior to all men; no one knows and no one could understand all that you think and all that you feel; they would even be incapable of appreciating the benevolence that they inspire in you. You are a king whom passers-by fail to recognise, and who lives in the solitude of his conviction: but what does that matter to you? Do you not possess that sovereign contempt which renders the soul so kindly?'

However, we can imagine that from time to time a caustic memory flickers up and corrodes this happiness. A suggestion provided by external circumstances can revivify a past that is unpleasant to contemplate. With how many stupid or vile actions is the past not filled, all of them quite unworthy of this king of thought, and sullying his ideal dignity? Believe me, the man on hashish will courageously confront these reproachful phantoms, and will even be able to derive from these hideous memories new occasions of pleasure and pride. This is how his train of thought will develop: once the first sensation of pain has passed, he will analyse with curiosity that action or that feeling the memory of which has intruded on his present glorification, the motives which made him act that way at the time, the circumstances in which he found himself, and, if he does not find in these circumstances sufficient reasons, if not to absolve at least to attenuate his sin, don't for a minute think he feels beaten! I can follow his reasoning as if watching the play of a mechanism behind a transparent pane of glass: 'That ridiculous, cowardly, or vile action, the memory of which disturbed me for a moment, is in complete contradiction with my real nature, my present nature, and the very energy with which I condemn that action, the inquisitorial care with which I analyse and judge it, proves my high and divine aptitude for virtue. How many men could be found throughout the world as skilled in self-judgement and as severe in self-condemnation?' And not only does he condemn himself, he glorifies himself. The horrible memory is thus absorbed into the contemplation of an ideal virtue, an ideal charity, an ideal genius, and he candidly gives himself up to his triumphant spiritual orgy. We have seen that, sacrilegiously counterfeiting the sacrament of penitence, at once penitent and confessor, he had granted himself a facile absolution, or, even worse, that he had drawn from his condemnation new matter for his pride to feast upon. Now, from the contemplation of his dreams and his virtuous plans, he concludes that he has a practical aptitude for virtue; the amorous energy with which he embraces this phantom of virtue appears to him a sufficient and conclusive proof of the virile energy necessary for accomplishing his ideal. He completely confuses dream with action, and as his imagination becomes more and more heated at the enchanting spectacle of his own corrected and idealised nature, substituting this fascinating image of himself for his real individual character – so poor in will-power, so rich in vanity – he finishes by decreeing his apotheosis in these clear and simple terms, which contain for him a whole world of abominable pleasures: 'I am the most virtuous of all men!'

Doesn't this remind you of Jean-Jacques, who, also, after confessing to the universe, not without a certain voluptuousness, dared utter the same cry of triumph (or at least there is very little difference between them), with the same sincerity and the same conviction? The enthusiasm with which he admired virtue, the highly strung way he would be moved to tears at the sight of a fine action or the thought of all the fine actions he would like to have performed, were enough to give him a superlative idea of his moral value. Jean-Jacques had become intoxicated without hashish.

Shall I take the analysis of this victorious monomania any further? Shall I explain how in the thrall of the poison, my man soon turns himself into the centre of the universe? How he becomes the living and caricatural expression of the proverb which says that passion relates everything back to itself? He believes in his virtue and his genius; can't you guess at how it will end? All the objects surrounding him are so many suggestions arousing in him a world of thoughts, all of them more brightly coloured, more vivid, more subtle than ever, and covered with a magical veneer. 'Those magnificent cities,' he says to himself, 'where the superb buildings are spaced out as in stage-sets – those fine ships swaying on the waves of the harbour in a nostalgic listlessness, which seem to be a translation of our thought, "When will we set sail for happiness?" – those museums crammed with beautiful shapes and intoxicating colours – those libraries in which are accumulated the labours of Science and the dreams of the Muse – those collections of instruments which speak with a single voice – those enchanting women, made more charming still by the science of adornment and their deliberate glances – all of those things have been created *for me, for me, for me!* For me has humanity laboured, been martyred and immolated – to serve as fodder, as pabulum for my implacable appetite for emotion, for knowledge and beauty!' I'm skipping and abbreviating a few passages. No one will be surprised that a final, supreme thought springs forth from the dreamer's brain: '*I have become God!*', or that a savage, ardent cry leaps from his breast with such energy, such power of projection that, if the desires and the beliefs of a drunken man had any efficacious virtue, this cry would overthrow the angels scattered across the paths of heaven: 'I am a god!' But soon this hurricane of pride is transformed into a climate of calm, mute, reposeful bliss, and the totality of all beings in the universe presents itself in many colours, seemingly illumined by a sulphurous dawn. If by chance a vague memory slips into the soul of this blissful wretch – 'Might there not be another god?' – take my word, he will stand boldly up before *that one*, will argue over his intentions and confront him without terror. Which French philosopher was it who, to mock modern German doctrines, said: 'I am a god with indigestion?' A hashish-intoxicated mind would be quite immune to this irony; he would tranquilly reply: 'It's possible that I have indigestion, but I am a god'.

5

E T H I C S

But the day after! The terrible day after! All your limp and exhausted organs, your slack nerves, the itching desire to weep, the impossibility of applying yourself to any continuous work, all teach you cruelly that you have been playing a forbidden game. Hideous nature, stripped of the illumination of the night before, resembles the melancholic debris after a feast. The will especially is attacked, the most precious of all faculties. They say, and it is almost true, that this substance causes no physical harm, nothing serious, at least. But can it be affirmed that a man incapable of action, and only good at dreaming, is really healthy, even if all his limbs are in good shape? For we are acquainted with human nature well enough to know that a man who can with a spoonful of jelly procure for himself instantaneously all that heaven and earth can offer, will never acquire the thousandth part of it by work. Can you imagine a state in which all the citizens get intoxicated with hashish? What citizens! what warriors! what legislators! Even in the Orient, where its use is so widespread, there are governments which have realised the necessity of banning it. Indeed, it is forbidden to man, on pain of degradation and intellectual death, to disturb the primordial conditions of his existence, and to destroy the equilibrium between his faculties and the environments in which they are designed to operate; in short, he is forbidden to disturb his destiny and replace it by a fate of a new kind. Let us remember Melmoth, that admirable emblem. His dreadful suffering resides in the disproportion between his marvellous faculties, acquired instantaneously through a satanic pact, and the environment in which, as a creature of God, he is condemned to live. And none of those he tries to seduce consents to buy from him, on the same conditions, his terrible privilege. Indeed, any man who does not accept the conditions of his life sells his soul. It is easy to grasp the relation existing between the satanic creatures of the poets and the living creatures who have devoted themselves to stimulants. Man has tried to become God, and soon we see him, by virtue of an implacable moral law, fallen lower than his real nature. He is a soul which sells itself piecemeal.

Balzac doubtless thought that there is no greater shame and no more intense suffering for man than the abdication of his will. I saw him once, at a gathering where the tremendous effects of hashish were being discussed. He was listening and asking questions with an amusing attentiveness and vivacity. People who have met him can easily guess how interested he must have been. But the idea of not being in control of his ideas shocked him intensely. He was offered some *dawamesk*;

he examined it, sniffed it, and handed it back without trying it. The struggle between his almost infantile curiosity and his repugnance for the abdication of the will was laid strikingly bare by his expressive face. The love of dignity won the day. Indeed, it is difficult to imagine the theorist of the will, that spiritual twin brother of Louis Lambert[6], consenting to lose the smallest portion of that precious *substance*.

Despite the admirable services rendered by ether and chloroform, it seems to me that from the point of view of spiritualist philosophy, the same moral blemish affects all modern inventions which tend to diminish human freedom and unavoidable pain. It is not without a certain admiration that I once heard the paradoxical comments of an officer telling me of the cruel operation performed on a French general at El-Aghouat, from which he died despite chloroform. This general was a really brave man, and even something more than that – one of those souls to whom can naturally be applied the term 'chivalrous'. 'It wasn't,' he told me, 'chloroform that he needed, but the gaze of the whole army and the music of the regiments. Then, perhaps, he might have been saved!' The surgeon didn't share this officer's opinion, but the chaplain would doubtless have admired these sentiments.

It is really superfluous, after all these considerations, to insist on the immoral character of hashish. If I compare it to suicide, to a slow suicide, a weapon always dripping with blood and always sharp, no reasonable mind will object. If I liken it to sorcery and magic, both of which seek, by operating on matter, and by arcane means whose falsity cannot be proved any more than their efficacy, to conquer a domain forbidden to man or permitted only to the man judged worthy, no philosophical soul will criticise this comparison. If the

Church condemns magic and sorcery, it is because they countermand God's intentions, suppress the labour of time and try to render superfluous the conditions of purity and morality; and because she, the Church, considers as legitimate and true only the treasures won by assiduous good intentions. We call a crook any gambler who has found a means of winning every time; what shall we call the man who seeks to purchase, with a small outlay, happiness and genius? It is the very infallibility of the means which constitutes its immorality, just as the supposed infallibility of magic sets its infernal mark on it. Should I add that hashish, like all solitary joys, makes a man useless to other men, and society superfluous to the individual, impelling him to admire himself ceaselessly and propelling him day by day towards the gleam of the abyss in which he may admire his face like Narcissus?

But what if, at the price of his dignity, his decency and his free will, man could derive from hashish great spiritual benefits, make of it a kind of thinking machine, a productive instrument? This is a question I have often heard asked, and I will answer it. First, as I have explained at length, hashish reveals to the individual nothing but the individual himself. It is true that this individual is, so to speak, raised to the third power and intensified to an extreme, and as it is also certain that the memory of impressions outlasts the orgy, the hope of these utilitarians does not appear at first sight to be altogether devoid of reason. But I would request them to observe that the thoughts from which they expect to derive such great benefit are not really as beautiful as they appear in their momentary disguise, draped with magical faded finery. They come from earth rather than heaven, and owe a great part of their beauty to the nervous agitation and the avidity with which our minds throw themselves upon them. And then, this hope is a vicious circle: let us admit for a moment that hashish gives you genius, or at least increases genius already there; they forget that it is in the nature of hashish to diminish will-power, and that it therefore gives with one hand what it takes away with the other: in other words it gives us imagination without the faculty of being able to benefit from it. Finally we have to remember, even if we may suppose a man adroit and vigorous enough to sidestep this alternative, another danger, fateful and terrible, the danger attached to all habits. They are all soon transformed into necessities. The man who resorts to a poison *in order to* think will soon no longer be able to think *without* the poison. Can you imagine the dreadful fate of a man whose paralysed imagination can no longer function without the aid of hashish or opium?

In philosophical studies, the human mind, imitating the course of the stars, must follow a curve which brings us back to its point of departure. To conclude is to close a circle. At the beginning I spoke of that wonderful state, in which the mind of man sometimes found itself thrown as if by a special grace; I said that in his ceaseless aspiration to rekindle his hopes and raise himself to the infinite, he showed, in all countries and at all times, a frenzied taste for all substances, even dangerous ones, which, by exalting his personality, could bring vividly to his eyes that second-hand paradise, the object of all his desires; and I finally claimed that this foolhardy mind, pushing on all unknowingly to hell, bore witness thereby to its own original greatness. But man is not so abandoned, so deprived of the honest means of winning heaven that he is forced to call on pharmacy and sorcery; he does not need to sell his soul to pay for the intoxicating caresses and friendship of houris. What is the paradise that you purchase at the cost of your eternal soul? I can imagine a man (shall I say a Brahman, a poet, or a Christian philosopher?) who has climbed the arduous Olympus of spirituality; around him the Muses of Raphael or Mantegna, to console him for his long periods of fasting and his unremitting prayers, weave the noblest dances, and gaze at him with their gentlest expressions and their most dazzling smiles; the divine Apollo, that master of all knowledge (the Apollo of Francavilla, Albrecht Dürer, Goltzius[7], or any other, what does it matter? Isn't there an Apollo for every man who deserves one?), produces with the strokes of his bow his most vibrant chords. Below him, at the foot of the mountain, in the briars and the mud, the troop of human beings, the band of serfs, simulate the grimaces of pleasure and utter the yells torn from them by the bite of the poison; and the saddened poet says to himself: 'Those unfortunates who have neither fasted nor prayed, and who have refused redemption through work, seek from black magic the means of raising themselves all at once to a supernatural existence. Magic deceives them and sheds on them the gleam of a false happiness and a false light; while we, poets and philosophers, we have regenerated our souls by sustained labour and contemplation. By the assiduous exercise of our will and the permanent nobility of our intentions, we have created for our use a garden of true beauty. Trusting in the word which says that faith can move mountains, we have accomplished the only miracle for which God has granted us permission!'

1. *Lazare* (*Lazarus*) is by the poet Auguste Barbier (1805–1879).

2. Joseph von Hammer-Purgstall (1774–1856), an Austrian orientalist, wrote a *History of the Assassins* (in German: 1818); Sylvestre de Sacy (1758–1838) was a French orientalist.

3. The Theatre of Séraphin is the name of a Parisian shadow and puppet theatre for children.

4. The French philosopher Blaise Pascal (1623–62) wrote, in his *Pensées* (*Thoughts*): 'Man is neither angel nor beast, and it is an unfortunate fact that whoever tries to be an angel ends up a beast'.

5. Baudelaire's translations of Poe are still the standard French version. The stories referred to here (I quote Poe's original English) are, respectively: 'Ligeia'; 'Berenice'; and 'A Tale of the Ragged Mountains'.

6. *Louis Lambert* is a novel by Balzac (1835) which, like *The Wild Ass's Skin*, deals with the notion that will-power is a physical substance.

7. Pierre Francheville (1548–*c.*1615), also known as Francavilla, was a French sculptor and architect; Albrecht Dürer (1471–1528) was a German engraver and painter; and Hendrik Goltzius (1558–1617) was a Dutch engraver and painter.

The dedicatory letter introducing *Artificial Paradises:*

To J.G.F.

My dear friend,

Common sense tells us that the things of the earth have hardly any existence, and that true reality is found only in dreams. In order to digest natural happiness, like the artificial variety, one must first have the courage to swallow it, and those who would perhaps deserve happiness are precisely those on whom felicity, as mortals conceive it, has always had the effect of an emetic.

To foolish minds it will seem strange, and even impertinent, that a picture of artificial pleasures should be dedicated to a woman, the most usual source of the most natural pleasures. And yet it is obvious that just as the natural world overlaps with the spiritual world and provides it with its raw material, thereby helping to create that indefinable amalgam that we call our individuality, woman is the being who casts the greatest shadow or sheds the greatest light onto our dreams. Woman is inevitably suggestive; she lives out another life than her own; she lives spiritually in the imaginations that she haunts and fertilises.

Besides, it is of really little importance whether the reason behind this dedication is understood. Is it even necessary, for the contentment of the author, that any book be understood, except by the man or the woman for whom it has been composed? To tell the whole truth, in fact, is it indispensable that the book should have been written for *anyone*? I have, for my part, so little liking for the living world that, similar to those sensitive women with time on their hands who, it is said, post their confidences to imaginary friends, I would be happy to write only for the dead.

But it is not to a dead woman that I am dedicating this little book; it is to one who, although ill, is still active and living within me, and who is now turning all her gazes towards heaven, that place of all transfigurations. For, just as much as a man enjoys a powerful drug, he enjoys the privilege of being able to derive new and subtle pleasures even from pain, catastrophe and fate.

You will see in this picture a sombre and solitary man out for a walk, immersed in the moving flood of the multitude, and sending his heart and his thought to a distant Electra who once wiped his sweat-bathed brow and brought refreshment to his lips shrivelled by fever; and you will guess at the gratitude of another Orestes whose nightmares you have often observed, and whose terrible slumbers you dispersed with a light and maternal hand.

– Charles Baudelaire

BIOGRAPHICAL NOTE

Charles-Pierre Baudelaire was born in Paris in 1821 to an elderly father and a much younger mother. His father imbued him with an appreciation of art, but died when Baudelaire was only six years of age. His mother remarried a year later, despatching the young Baudelaire to boarding-schools in both Lyon and Paris. Expelled at eighteen without having taken his *baccalauréat*, Baudelaire then enrolled in law school. By this time he had contracted syphilis – a disease from which he would suffer for the rest of his life. In 1842, Baudelaire gained his inheritance, yet his extravagant lifestyle led his family to transfer control of his finances to a notary in 1844, and he thereafter lived on an allowance and on loans.

Baudelaire's writing career began in earnest in the 1840s, with early art criticism reviewing the annual Paris art exhibitions. *Salons de Paris* (1845, 46), his second work, in particular, proved to be a ground-breaking aesthetic treatise. In 1846 a novella entitled *La Fanfarlo* appeared; two years later amid Republican fervour he edited two short-lived Socialist journals; and by the early 1850s was translating the *Tales* of Edgar Allan Poe – presumably attracted by Poe's themes of beauty, death, and the bizarre. He was also at work on *Les Fleurs du Mal*, which, though it led to legal proceedings concerning the questionable morality of six of the 101 poems in the volume when it appeared in 1857, is now thought to be possibly the most influential collection of poetry published in Europe in the nineteenth century.

A revised, expanded edition of *Les Fleurs du Mal* appeared in 1861, entitled *Petits poèmes en prose* (*Le spleen de Paris*), in which Baudelaire continued his series of prose poems detailing his 'spleen' or moods of isolation and despair.

Following a disastrous lecture-tour in Belgium where he remained until 1866, he suffered paralysis to one side of his body and aphasia. He returned to Paris where he died a year later.

Andrew Brown studied at the University of Cambridge, where he taught French for many years. He now works as a freelance teacher and translator. He is the author of *Roland Barthes: the Figures of Writing* (OUP, 1992), and various translations of works relating to French history and philosophy.

HESPERUS PRESS CLASSICS

Hesperus Press, as suggested by the Latin motto, is committed to bringing near what is far – far both in space and time. Works written by the greatest authors, and unjustly neglected or simply little known in the English-speaking world, are made accessible through new translations and a completely fresh editorial approach. Through these classic works, the reader is introduced to the greatest writers from all times and all cultures.

For more information on Hesperus Press, please visit our website: **www.hesperuspress.com**

ET REMOTISSIMA PROPE

SELECTED TITLES FROM HESPERUS PRESS

Author	Title	Foreword writer
Pietro Aretino	*The School of Whoredom*	Paul Bailey
Pietro Aretino	*The Secret Life of Nuns*	
Jane Austen	*Lesley Castle*	Zoë Heller
Jane Austen	*Love and Friendship*	Fay Weldon
Honoré de Balzac	*Colonel Chabert*	A.N. Wilson
Charles Baudelaire	*On Wine and Hashish*	Margaret Drabble
Giovanni Boccaccio	*Life of Dante*	A.N. Wilson
Charlotte Brontë	*The Spell*	
Emily Brontë	*Poems of Solitude*	Helen Dunmore
Mikhail Bulgakov	*Fatal Eggs*	Doris Lessing
Mikhail Bulgakov	*The Heart of a Dog*	A.S. Byatt
Giacomo Casanova	*The Duel*	Tim Parks
Miguel de Cervantes	*The Dialogue of the Dogs*	Ben Okri
Geoffrey Chaucer	*The Parliament of Birds*	
Anton Chekhov	*The Story of a Nobody*	Louis de Bernières
Anton Chekhov	*Three Years*	William Fiennes
Wilkie Collins	*The Frozen Deep*	
Joseph Conrad	*Heart of Darkness*	A.N. Wilson
Joseph Conrad	*The Return*	Colm Tóibín
Gabriele D'Annunzio	*The Book of the Virgins*	Tim Parks
Dante Alighieri	*The Divine Comedy: Inferno*	
Dante Alighieri	*New Life*	Louis de Bernières
Daniel Defoe	*The King of Pirates*	Peter Ackroyd
Marquis de Sade	*Incest*	Janet Street-Porter
Charles Dickens	*The Haunted House*	Peter Ackroyd
Charles Dickens	*A House to Let*	
Fyodor Dostoevsky	*The Double*	Jeremy Dyson
Fyodor Dostoevsky	*Poor People*	Charlotte Hobson
Alexandre Dumas	*One Thousand and One Ghosts*	

Francis Petrarch	*My Secret Book*	Germaine Greer
Luigi Pirandello	*Loveless Love*	
Edgar Allan Poe	*Eureka*	Sir Patrick Moore
Alexander Pope	*The Rape of the Lock* and *A Key to the Lock*	Peter Ackroyd
Antoine-François Prévost	*Manon Lescaut*	Germaine Greer
Marcel Proust	*Pleasures and Days*	A.N. Wilson
Alexander Pushkin	*Dubrovsky*	Patrick Neate
Alexander Pushkin	*Ruslan and Lyudmila*	Colm Tóibín
François Rabelais	*Pantagruel*	Paul Bailey
François Rabelais	*Gargantua*	Paul Bailey
Christina Rossetti	*Commonplace*	Andrew Motion
George Sand	*The Devil's Pool*	Victoria Glendinning
Jean-Paul Sartre	*The Wall*	Justin Cartwright
Friedrich von Schiller	*The Ghost-seer*	Martin Jarvis
Mary Shelley	*Transformation*	
Percy Bysshe Shelley	*Zastrozzi*	Germaine Greer
Stendhal	*Memoirs of an Egotist*	Doris Lessing
Robert Louis Stevenson	*Dr Jekyll and Mr Hyde*	Helen Dunmore
Theodor Storm	*The Lake of the Bees*	Alan Sillitoe
Leo Tolstoy	*The Death of Ivan Ilych*	
Leo Tolstoy	*Hadji Murat*	Colm Tóibín
Ivan Turgenev	*Faust*	Simon Callow
Mark Twain	*The Diary of Adam and Eve*	John Updike
Mark Twain	*Tom Sawyer, Detective*	
Oscar Wilde	*The Portrait of Mr W.H.*	Peter Ackroyd
Virginia Woolf	*Carlyle's House and Other Sketches*	Doris Lessing
Virginia Woolf	*Monday or Tuesday*	Scarlett Thomas
Emile Zola	*For a Night of Love*	A.N. Wilson